M000303644

IROQUOIS

THEIR ART and CRAFTS

EDITOR'S NOTE

This book was originally published as *Iroquois Crafts* by Carrie A. Lyford in 1945. For the Hancock House edition, the text has been updated into a more modern style, and the subject matter has been reorganized into new chapter headings. New photographs and diagrams have been selected, and a color section has been added. The basic information contained in the text, however, has been retained, as the subject matter of this book deals primarily with the technology and skills of the Iroquois, both pre- and post-contact.

Lisa Smedman, Editor

IROQUOIS
Their Art
and Crafts

Carrie A. Lyford

hancock

house

ISBN 0-88839-135-8
Copyright © 1989 Carrie Lyford

Canadian Cataloging in Publication Data
    Lyford, Carrie
        Iroquois, their art and crafts
Originally published: Washington, D.C.:
U.S. Bureau of Indian Affairs, 1945, under
title: Iroquois crafts.

1. Iroquois Indians.   I. Title.   II. Title: Iroquois
crafts.

E99.I7L9 1985   970.004'97   082-091165-8

All rights reserved. No part of this publication may be
reproduced, stored in a retrieval system or transmitted,
in any form or by any means, electronic, mechanical,
photocopying, recording or otherwise, without the
prior written permission of Hancock House Publishers.

Printed in Hong Kong

Published simultaneously in Canada and the United States by

HANCOCK HOUSE PUBLISHERS LTD.
19313 Zero Ave., Surrey, B.C. V3S 5J9
HANCOCK HOUSE PUBLISHERS
1431 Harrison Avenue, Blaine, WA 98230

CONTENTS

Chief Johnson Williams and family, Grand River, Ontario.
Photo: F.W. Waugh, 1912.

INTRODUCTION
History of the Iroquois

There is nothing more colorful in North American Indian history than the story of the League of the Iroquois. These five (and later six) tribes or nations were welded into a powerful confederacy about 1570 under founder and lawgiver Hiawatha. The Iroquois tribes had been weakened by continuous intertribal wars and conflict with the Algonquin, so the league was formed for the double purpose of acquiring strength and establishing and enforcing peace. The tribes that formed the League expected all other nations to acknowledge the League's supremacy and join it beneath the symbolic peace tree.

The League of the Iroquois was governed by a carefully worked out constitution that was transmitted orally from one generation to another by lords or sachems, who were selected to learn and recite the laws and regulations. For many generations the details of the constitution were recorded in a collection of wampum belts and strings, twenty-five of which were preserved in the New York State Museum.

In spite of the ideal of peace, the history of the League was one of intertribal warfare, particularly during the seventeenth century. The members of the League showed themselves to be fierce and formidable fighters. They obtained firearms from the Dutch with whom they came in contact early in the century, and they developed a power that made them the scourge of Indian tribes from the Atlantic to the Mississippi, and from Ottawa to Tennessee.

They are known to have penetrated as far west as the Black Hills and to have attacked the Catawba in South Carolina and the Creek in Florida. Much of the western movement of the Iroquois was as a result of the fur trade. With the beaver depleted in their own area, the Iroquois followed the fur trading companies into new regions.

The golden age of the League was from 1650 to 1755, after which its power declined. In the eighteenth century, tribal locations and movements were determined by French and British colonial policies in the struggle for control of the continent by these nations.

The members of the League were called the "Iroquois" by the French, the "Five Nations" by the English, and "men of men" or

7

"original men" by themselves. They came to the east from areas to the west and south about 1400, and settled in villages in the area that extends from west of the Hudson River to the Genesee, and from the Adirondacks south of the St. Lawrence River to the headwaters of the Susquehanna River. They represented only a fraction of the linguistically related tribes that formed the Iroquoian group. Other Iroquois tribes moved into Canada and south of the Chesapeake to the Carolinas, while outlying bands lived in Tennessee.

The five tribes or nations that made up the League included the Mohawk, who were the most easterly of the five tribes and who called themselves "the possessors of the flint"; the Oneida, "the granite people," or "the people of the standing stone"; the Onondaga, "the people on the hills," who took their name from their position on the top of the hill or mountain; the Cayuga, "the people at the marshy land"; and the Seneca or "the great hill people." In 1722 the Tuscarora, "the hemp gatherers," or "the shirt wearing people," who had come up from the Carolinas, joined the confederacy, and thereafter it became known as the "Six Nations."

The term "longhouse" was at one time symbolically applied to the League, and its members spoke of themselves as the *Hodinonhsio'-ni o'non*, "the people of the longhouse." The symbolic longhouse was represented as extending from the Hudson River to Lake Erie. It sheltered within its walls the five tribes who kept the five fires of the longhouse. At the ends of the house stood the doorkeepers, the Mohawk at the east and the Seneca at the west. In between these were the Oneida, who kept the second fire, and the Cayuga, who kept the fourth fire. They were regarded as the younger brothers whose duty it was to care for the captives. The Onondaga kept the ever-burning central fire and presided over the council of the league. Their principal village, Onondaga (later Onondaga Castle), was the capital of the confederacy. At one time Onondaga was one of the most important and widely known towns in North America north of Mexico. It is estimated that at the time of their greatest power, the Five Nations numbered between ten and fifteen thousand.

The Iroquois did not take part in the American Revolution as a league. Each nation decided upon its individual action in relation to the colonies. At the close of the war those who had supported Great Britain moved to lands in the province of Ontario assigned to them by the Crown. Many of the descendants of the original Iroquois now live in Canada.

Some time after the American Revolution, the Iroquois

remaining in the United States were recognized by this country as a nation, and the tribes were guaranteed peaceful possession of their reservations in New York state under the 1794 treaty of Canandaigua, and in subsequent treaties. Most of the Iroquois of the United States continue to live on the six major New York reservations, with the exception of the Oneida, who were moved westward and finally settled near Green Bay, Wisconsin, in 1846. The majority of the Iroquois in the state of New York belong to the Seneca and Mohawk tribes.

HABITAT
Villages

The Iroquois were a hunting, fishing, and agricultural people. They lived in compactly built villages consisting of twenty to one hundred houses built on high, level tracts of land, or on bluffs set back from streams or lakes. The villages were surrounded by small vegetable gardens, orchards, and cornfields of up to several hundred hectares. Around the time of the formation of the League (1570), villages were enclosed by a single or double row of palisades or stockades erected as protection from attack by hostile tribes. The stockades were made of five-meter-long logs, sharpened at one end and set in a continuous row in an earth embankment. In a

Typical Iroquois village with palisade.

National Museum of Man
National Museums of Canada
Neg. #J-4436

description of his travels (1535), Giambattista Ramusio tells of a strongly palisaded Iroquoian town known as Hochelaga where about 3,600 people lived in fifty houses, each built with a frame of thick poles covered with bark.

The need for village stockades had almost ceased by the beginning of the seventeenth century, and by the end of the century stockades were abandoned. Villages became less compact, but houses continued to be built near enough together to form a neighborhood.

It was sometimes necessary to change the village sites. The bark houses decayed and became unfit to live in, accessible firewood became exhausted, and the soil ceased to be productive. Moving to a new site and building up a village involved a great deal of work.

The Longhouse

The characteristic home of the Iroquois was a communal house made of log and bark known as the longhouse, designed to accommodate five, ten, or twenty families. The longhouse ranged from 9 to 60 meters in length, from 4½ to 7½ meters in width, and from 4½ to 6 meters in height at the center. The average longhouse was 18 meters in length and 5½ meters in width and height, and was built with a framework of upright posts with forked tops. The lower ends of the posts were set 30 centimeters into the ground to form a rectangular space the size of the building to be constructed. Horizontal poles were tied with flexible twigs to the vertical poles, along the sides and across the tops. A steep triangular or rounded roof was formed by bending the slender, flexible poles toward the center above the space enclosed by the poles.

The framework of logs was covered with bark gathered in the spring or early summer up to mid-July. Slabs of bark just over a meter wide and 2 to 2½ meters long were removed from the elm, hemlock, basswood, ash, or cedar trees. Elm bark was preferred. The bark slabs were pressed flat under weights, and laid horizontally over the framework of poles, overlapping one another like shingles. Basswood withes or strips of bast from the inner bark of basswood and hickory trees were used to fasten the pieces of bark together and to secure them to the framework. Holes for use in sewing were made in the bark using a bone puncher.

A series of poles corresponding to the poles of the framework were set up outside and close to the bark, on the four sides and across the roof. They were tied to the first set of poles to hold the bark firmly in place. No metal tools or commercially manufactured materials were used in longhouse construction.

The longhouse had no windows. Light came from the high, wide doors at each end, and from above. A movable piece of bark or tanned hide, which could be easily tied back, was used as a door at the entrance. Square openings in the roof admitted light and allowed smoke to escape. Pieces of bark were kept on the roof to close the holes in the event of wind, rain, or snow. They could be

:erior of an Iroquois longhouse, from a painting by R.J. Tucker.

National Museum of Man
National Museums of Canada
Neg. # 76024

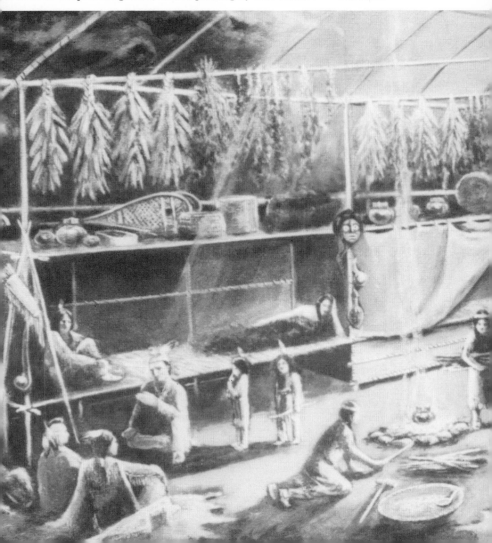

controlled from inside the building by pushing with a long pole.

Compartments or booths housing family groups were raised 45 centimeters from the ground along the two sides. The booths were from 2 to 2½ meters long and nearly 2 meters wide. They could be curtained off with skins to provide privacy. Each compartment belonged to a given family and was not accessible to members of other families. Thus, although housing was communal, private ownership existed.

Meter-wide platforms covered with several layers of bark, reed mats, and soft fur robes ran along the sides of the booths, and served as bunks for sleeping. Smaller bunks were sometimes built for children. Storage platforms were erected about two meters over the bunks, where cooking utensils, clothes, hunting equipment, and other possessions were kept.

Pits were often dug under the beds for storing family valuables. Large bundles of dried corn (joined by braiding the husks of the ears together), strips of dried pumpkin, strings of dried apples and squash, herbs, and other supplies were hung on the cross poles or rafters. Storage booths and platforms were provided for barrels and other large containers of food at each end of the longhouse.

Rough stone fireplaces along the central passage between the booths contained small fires for warmth, light, and cooking. One

12

Sourspring longhouse possibly dating to 1800. Photo: C.M. Barbeau, 1949

National Museum of Man
National Museums of Canada
Neg. # J-2937

house might have as many as twelve fires, each one shared by two families.

Around the time of the American Revolution, the Iroquois were using a variety of inventions in their bark-covered homes. Corn husk rugs, splint baskets, gourd containers, and skin bags were just a few examples. Braids of sweet grass were sometimes hung in a house to decorate and perfume it. A strong straight bough or a thick board that had been deeply notched up one side served as a ladder to provide access to the high platform and the roof.

The longhouse continued in use up to the eighteenth century, then was gradually abandoned.

Smaller Buildings

Single family six-meter-long houses of logs and elm bark came into use during the seventeenth century. These were replaced at the end of the century by houses of white pine logs, which were still used for storage up to the middle of the twentieth century. Today, small frame houses predominate on the reservations.

In the old days a small dome-shaped hut of bent saplings, about one meter high and two meters in diameter, was used for a sweat bath in the summer. Heated stones piled in the hut were covered with water poured from a bark container until clouds of steam surrounded the bather, producing a cleansing sweat. The bather was then rubbed with sand, and plunged into a nearby stream. These huts were still in use until sometime in the nineteenth century.

Single family dwelling.

13

SUBSISTENCE
Food Gathering and Preparation

Among the Iroquois, food gathering involved a division of labor; the women did the gardening, while the men were the hunters. In the early days the Iroquois utilized a great deal of both fresh and dried fish and meat. The many lakes and streams of their country yielded an abundant supply of fish during the spring fishing season. During the season of the fall hunt, the men set out on long and tiring expeditions to kill game. In lean times, the Iroquois found it necessary to supplement their diet with the meat of many of the smaller animals. In old village sites, bones of bison, deer, elk, black bear, porcupine, raccoon, martin, otter, woodchuck, muskrat, beaver, skunk, weasel, and dog have been found. Domestic pigs, geese, ducks, and chickens became sources of food after their introduction into Quebec about 1620.

After the formation of the League, when the Iroquois became settled in more permanent villages, their food supply depended increasingly on agricultural products, and domesticated foodstuffs began to constitute the major portion of their diet.

The entire process of planting, cultivating, harvesting, and

National Museum of Man
National Museums of Canada
Neg. # 17120

Cayuga Indian using a single-pronged fish-spear on the Six Nation Reservation. Photo: F.W. Waugh, 1912.

Department of Mines Geological Survey
Neg. # 17147

Iroquois fish trap in place across a stream.

preparing food for the family was in the hands of the women. An older woman was elected to direct the communal fields, where each woman cared for a designated portion. Certain fields were reserved for providing food for the councils and national feasts. Special songs were sung at the time of planting and harvesting, and ceremonial sacrifices of tobacco and wampum were made to spirits of the crops.

Through a mutual aid society the women assisted one another in their individual fields when planting, hoeing, and harvesting, singing while they worked. Each woman brought her own hoe, pail, and spoon. When the work was over, a feast was provided by the owner of the field, and everyone went home with a supply of food, usually corn soup and hominy (a mash of dried and ground corn, prepared by boiling in water or milk).

Corn has always been the principal food of the Iroquois. Corn pits have been found at old village sites. Even before the formation of the League, corn, beans, and squash were cultivated. Because these three vegetables were grown together they were sometimes called "the three sisters." The Iroquois spoke of them as "our life," or "our supporters." A number of myths and several ceremonies were centered around them.

Ears of mature corn were hung to dry inside and outside of the Iroquois home. Large quantities of corn were dried in corn cribs, built of unpainted planks in open-slat construction, through which air could circulate freely. The corn crib was a characteristic feature of the small farm on Iroquois reservations. Its use was adopted by

15

early North American settlers.

The corn used by the Iroquois was of two common types: white dent and white flint, with occasional red ears. The white dent corn, called Tuscarora or squaw corn, was hulled or eaten on the cob. Both green and mature corn were used in the preparation of many dishes. Green corn was boiled on the cob, roasted on the cob in the husk, scraped and baked, scraped and fried in cakes, combined with green beans and stewed with fat meat as succotash, used in a soup when green or dried, or scraped when green and baked in a loaf. Coarsely ground meal was made from either hulled or unhulled mature corn that was pounded in a stone or wooden mortar. It was used as plain mush, combined with meat, dressed with oil, or baked as unleavened bread.

Flint corn was used in making hominy. It was prepared by soaking shelled corn in lye until the hulls could be removed. Other flint corn dishes included hulled-corn soup, in which hulled corn was combined with beans and pork or beef, and boiled corn bread in which the hulled corn was usually combined with beans.

Charred corn was used throughout the year. Corn to be charred was selected when well along in the milky stage. The ears were set on end in a row before a long fire. Roasting continued until

Iroquois woman sifting meal.

National Museum of Man
National Museums of Canada
Neg. # 23912

National Museums of Canada
Neg. #17139

Cayuga Indians using mortar and pestle. Photo: F.W. Waugh, 1912.

the kernels were dry, then the corn was shelled and further dried in the sun. Charred corn was so reduced in bulk and weight that it could be easily stored or transported. If it was to be kept for some time, it was cached in earthen pits. It could be preserved for several years and was used both uncooked and cooked, or pounded fine and mixed with maple sugar. It was also made into cakes for use by hunters and warriors. In later years charred corn was used mainly at ceremonial functions.

The cultivation and use of several varieties of corn by the Iroquois required special tools and utensils for handling corn products. Every Iroquois home contained a mortar and pestle, a hulling basket, a hominy sieve basket, a netted scoop for removing ground corn from the mortar and for sifting out the coarser grains, a corn scraper, ladles, trays of bark and wood, and a long paddle for stirring corn soup and for removing the loaves from boiling water. The Mohawk used a soft hulling bag or basket in which the corn was twirled to remove the hulls after it had been boiled in lye.

Ten or more varieties of beans of different sizes, shapes, and colors were grown by the Iroquois. Since they did not use milk or cheese, beans were the only source of protein when meat was scarce. The beans used were commonly known as bush beans, wampum, purple and white kidney beans, marrow-fat beans, string, cornstalk, cranberry, chestnut, lima, hummingbird, white (small), wild peas, bean vines, and pole beans.

Beans were used alone to some extent but more often were combined with corn or squash when cooked. Beans were used as an ingredient in Iroquois corn bread.

17

Grinding corn in a large bowl, using a smooth stone. Photo: F.W. Waugh, 1912.

Mealing stone and miller.

National Museum of Man
National Museums of Canada
Neg. # 23930, 30808

Squashes and pumpkins, both fresh and dried for winter use, were always popular foods. Crook neck, hubbard, scalloped and winter squashes, hard pumpkins, artichokes and leeks, as well as corn and beans were grown. Wild cucumber, turnips, and edible fungi were also used as food. Sunflower oil was used in the preparation of many dishes.

Several varieties of berries were gathered by the Iroquois, although there is no evidence that they were ever cultivated. These included blackberries, blueberries, checkerberries, chokecherries, wild red cherries, cranberries, currants, dewberries, elderberries, gooseberries, hackberries, hawthorns, huckleberries, June or service berries, red mulberries, red and black raspberries, strawberries, and thimble berries. Small black plums, acorns, beechnuts, butternuts, chestnuts, hazelnuts, and hickory nuts were also eaten. By 1779, apples, peaches, pears, and cherries had been introduced from Europe. Muskmelons and watermelons were greatly used in later years. Fresh or dried berries were combined with hominy and corn bread to give added color and flavor.

Maple sugar was an important article of the diet and was used almost as much as salt is today. Maple sap was used as a beverage, either fresh or fermented. Salt was rarely used. The sunflower was grown in large quantities and its seed was used in herbal remedies.

Gourds and tobacco were also grown by the Iroquois. The gourds had many uses: as cups, dippers, spoons, and bowls in the home, and as rattles in ceremonies and dances. Tobacco had both secular and sacred uses. The Iroquois believed that tobacco was given to them as a means of communication with the spiritual world. By burning it they could make their requests known to the Great Spirit.

Iroquois men and some women smoked tobacco mixed with sumac leaves and red willow bark. Special tobaccos were used in ceremonies. Tobacco was cast on the waters, especially on falls and rapids, to pacify the spirits within, and was put in small bags attached to masks to make them more effective.

Shelling corn in preparation for stringing and storage. Photo: F.W. Waugh, 1912.

National Museum of Man
National Museums of Canada
Neg. # 23918, 30806

Husking pins and kernel scraper.

19

Cooking Techniques

Cooking fires were usually built in sunken pits where food was grilled in the flames, boiled in clay pots supported over the fire by stones or branches, or baked in hot ashes raked out of the fire. Strips of inner bark, the ends of which were folded together and tied around with a splint, formed an improvised emergency kettle. This bark kettle was suspended between two sticks over a fire and filled with water, into which meat was dropped. By the time the bark had burned through, the meat was cooked.

Much of the women's time was occupied with making clay pots for cooking. The characteristic extension rim on early Iroquois pots provided a ridge where a bark cord could be tied around the neck without slipping, so that the pot could be hung from forks of branches set, tripod fashion, over the fire. The rounded base made it possible for the pot to remain upright when set in the fire or in soft earth. With the coming of the colonists, kettles of copper, brass, and iron replaced the baked clay pots. Later, cook stoves took the place of the cooking fire.

Fire had many uses, including hollowing out wooden canoes and mortars, felling large trees that were to be used for buildings, and domestic uses such as cooking and heating.

In pre-colonial days the Iroquois started fire by a bow and shaft

Bow and shaft or pump drill being used to ignite tinder.

Department of Mines Geological Survey
Neg. # 17403

or pump drill. It consisted of a weighted upright stick or spindle of resinous wood about three centimeters thick and forty-five centimeters to over a meter in length. A leather thong or string attached to the ends of a meter-long bow was tied to the top of the spindle, and a small wheel was set upon the lower part of the shaft to give it momentum. The base of the spindle was inserted in a notch in a piece of very dry wood, near which a piece of frayed rope (tow) or decayed wood (punk) was placed.

When ready to use, the string was first coiled around the shaft by turning it by hand, then the bow was pulled down quickly, uncoiling the string and spinning the shaft. The momentum of the wheel recoiled the string, and the bow was drawn upwards. The bow was then pulled downward again, spinning the shaft in the opposite direction, uncoiling the string, and recoiling it as before. This alternating spinning motion of the shaft was continued until the friction created by the spindle ignited the powdered wood surrounding it. This was used to light kindling which had been placed nearby.

Preservation and Storage of Food

The Iroquois built shelters for their farm and garden equipment, and cribs in which corn could be dried and kept. They dug underground pits or caches for the storage of corn and other foods in the dry season, lining the bottom and sides with bark. A watertight bark roof was constructed over it, then the entire structure was covered with earth.

Corn, beans, berries, and other fruits were dried for winter use. Braided strings of corn were hung beside long spirals of dried squash and pumpkin outside the shelter, or from the rafters inside. Charred and dried shelled corn was kept in bark barrels buried in pits. Pits of well-preserved corn have been found near ancient village sites.

Bark barrels were of all sizes, with a capacity ranging from nine to over one hundred liters. They were made of black ash bark with the grain running around the barrel, and were stitched up the side and provided with a tight-fitting base and lid. In addition to storing corn, the barrels were also used to store beans, dried fruits, venison and other meats, articles of clothing, and accessories. Surplus meat and fish were dried, smoked, or frozen for later use and stored in bark barrels lined with deer skins.

TECHNOLOGY

Evidence of pre-contact technology has been found in New York State in middens, which provide the archaeologist with artifacts of stone, clay, antler, bone, and other well-preserved materials. Existing collections of early Indian pottery and beautifully carved wooden utensils testify to the artistic skill attained in prehistoric times. Almost nothing remains, however, of the weaving, braiding, and embroidery made of more perishable materials, and there is little on which to base a study of the pre-contact techniques and designs in these media.

In 1609, the Dutch found the Iroquois manufacturing a number of products: net, twine, and rope from elm, cedar, and basswood bark; ceremonial baskets, mats, dolls, moccasins, masks, belts, and burden straps from vegetable fibers and buffalo hairs; tanned hide clothing decorated with moose hair, porcupine quills, shells, and native beads; dishes and spoons of bark; carved wooden ladles, spoons, masks, and bows and arrows; and pots and pipes of clay. Many of these activities ceased after contact with white settlers and the introduction of European goods.

Traditionally, Iroquois men and women had different areas of activity. Men were occupied in hunting, fishing, and waging war. They built the longhouse and the palisades, made the canoes and paddles, mortars and pestles, snowshoes, lacrosse sticks, war clubs, pipes, bark and wooden dishes, and other wooden implements. They also carved the ritualistic wooden masks. Usually the men helped to gather the materials for handicraft work and assisted the women in clearing the land and harvesting the crops, though in the early days they shunned field work. As warfare and hunting decreased, the men assisted to a greater extent with farm work.

Iroquois women made ropes and cords of elm and basswood bark; sewed clothing; made baskets, sieves, and pottery vessels; did the weaving and embroidery; carried on the agricultural work; gathered firewood, roots, berries, fruit, and nuts; smoked and dried the fish and game; carried the burdens on the expeditions; and tanned hides with the help of the men.

With the coming of the traders, the domestic life of the Iroquois was revolutionized. Certain articles were inspired by the introduction of manufactured goods, including beads, yarns, colored silks and broadcloths, knives, needles, and other metal tools. The production

22

of some of the original native articles ceased altogether, such as pottery and skin clothing. Iroquois artifacts as we know them show European influence in form and design, though to a considerable extent the techniques used continued to be based on those developed in pre-contact times. Fortunately, much can be learned of the early life and activities of the Iroquois from well-illustrated descriptions written during the latter half of the nineteenth century, and from museum collections.

Antler, Stone, and Bone Tools

The pre-contact Iroquois utilized a variety of implements made of antler, stone, and bone. Decorative designs were incised on many of the articles with chert (rockflint) blades.

Antlers were used for tools and ornaments such as knife handles, digging blades, awls, punches, combs, wedges, spoons, needles, and fish hooks.

Stone adzes and axes in various shapes, sizes, and weights were used in working with charred wood when hollowing canoes, mortars, and other containers. Stone mortars were used for pounding corn, for grinding ingredients for mineral paint, and for pulverizing roots and barks for medicine. Rounded cobblestones were used for mullers or pounders. Some of the stone mortars were so small that they could easily be carried in a basket. Axes, bannerstones, bone blades, grinding stones, stone gouges, hammerstones, and notched stone sinkers are found in large numbers in old Iroquoian sites.

The Iroquois excelled in the manufacture of bone instruments. The bones of many animals and birds were used, including those of

Chipped-stone blades.

National Museum of Man
National Museums of Canada
Neg. # 30807

23

the deer, elk, moose, bear, buffalo, duck, turkey, goose, heron, and other large water birds. Awls, long narrow knives, gouges, arrow points, fish hooks, harpoons, needles, shuttles, and many other objects were made from bone. The flat shoulder bone of a deer, or a tortoise shell sharpened upon a stone and fastened to a short stick, made a hoe.

Bones were also popular for decorative purposes. Hundreds of tiny bone beads, which were perforated and strung as necklaces, have been found. Bone combs from as early as the seventeenth century have survived fairly well, although the teeth are often broken. At first the combs were simple in design, with only a few strong teeth. Many later were carved to show figures of men, birds, and animals, and were decorated with line designs.

Weapons

Iroquois men devised a number of effective weapons. The making of spears, bows and arrows, and the tomahawk or war club occupied much of their time. Weapons were constantly being broken, lost, or worn out and had to be replaced, creating a steady demand.

Spear points found on very early Iroquoian sites reveal the work of master craftsmen. Their delicate chipping, symmetry, and splendid notching make them among the most beautiful specimens of lithic art. The large points varied in size, shape, and notching, and were fastened to the ends of wooden shafts or handles. These were used in warfare, hunting and fishing, and at ceremonies.

The arrowhead, or arrow point, was thought to have evolved from the spear point. Arrowheads were made of a variety of stone, including chert, yellow jasper, quartz, hornstone, diabase, arkillite, chalcedony, and slate. They varied in size and shape, but the greatest number of Iroquois arrowheads were triangular, delicately

Use of the bow and arrow while seated. Photo: F.W. Waugh, 1912.

National Museums of Canada
Neg. # 17174

chipped from chert. Except for a few long, slender types, arrowheads were usually less than four centimeters in length.

Sheaths or quivers for bows and arrows were woven of corn husks, or made of bark or skin decorated with quill designs. In their early history, wooden shields protected the Iroquois from spears and arrows.

The Iroquois war club was originally a heavy weapon sixty centimeters in length made of ironwood. The rounded head, twelve to fifteen centimeters in diameter, sometimes resembled a human face or a ball enclosed by claws. War clubs were also made with a fine piece of flint, bone, or stone attached to the end, or a deer horn inserted in the edge. Through trade with colonists, brass, steel, and iron war clubs replaced the wooden ones. When no longer used in warfare, the war club continued to have a place in ceremonial observances.

Mohawk war club of ironwood and stone.

National Museum of Man
National Museums of Canada
Neg. # 21503

The tomahawk, which the Iroquois could throw with great accuracy, was originally a stone weapon similar to an axe. A deep groove was cut around the outside of the stone, to which a wooden handle was attached with a willow withe or a rawhide thong. Sometimes the tomahawk was brightly painted and decorated with beadwork, feathers, fur, and hair. When iron began to be used for tomahawk blades, these weapons were constructed to be alternately used as pipes. A bowl protruded from the flat back of the blade, and the wooden handle was hollowed out to allow smoke to pass through.

Iroquois tomahawks. Blades are of chipped stone or of horn, lashed onto a wooden handle with leather thongs.

National Museum of Man
National Museums of Canada
Neg. # 95019

Shell Tools and Ornaments

The Iroquois used shell for both utilitarian and ornamental purposes. Thin, sharp edges made shells good cutting, scraping, and digging tools. Their concave shape made them useful as cups, spoons, and bowls, and their delicate coloring and attractive texture made them valuable for personal ornamentation and decoration.

Pottery

At the beginning of the eighteenth century, the Iroquois method of pottery making was widely practiced. The early pottery was strong and fine, resembling that of the Cherokee. As contact with whites increased, pottery quality began to deteriorate. Soon, Iroquois pottery was replaced by large iron and brass kettles from Europe.

Traditionally, cooking was done in clay pots. The typical Iroquois clay pot had a spherical body with a rounded bottom, a narrow or constricted neck, and a projecting rim ornamented with incised or carved triangular designs. A border of elongated notches ran around the lower edge of the rim and sometimes produced raised points. In some cases the rim was omitted, the neck was short, and the top edge was notched, indented, knobbed, or scalloped. Most pottery was the color of the fired clay, but some black varieties could take on a high polish.

Iroquois pottery was made by the coiling process. Carefully selected clay was powdered and mixed with a tempering material such as pulverized quartz, stone, shell, or sand to prevent cracking. It was then moistened and kneaded like bread dough. The prepared clay was rolled intb ropes, which were kept moist. The clay ropes were coiled upon a saucerlike base, where they were worked into the desired shape. The ropes were sometimes coiled around a gourd, which helped to produce a symmetrical form. The gourd could be turned to make the inside smooth. As it could not be removed after the neck of the pot was formed, it was left in to burn away during the firing process. The clay ropes or coils were pressed together with a wet paddle or smoothing stone that was first dipped in water. A collar, sometimes round, but more often four-sided with an upward turn at each corner, was then formed and fitted to the neck.

Line decorations were used on the collar. Triangular plots of parallel lines were incised or drawn in the clay, and their direction changed in each adjoining plot. Impressions of fingernails, corn cobs, and a cord-wrapped stick were used as decoration. Human faces and figures were used in decoration for nearly fifty years in the late sixteenth and early seventeenth centuries. Figures were often drawn at the corners of the neck or rim with three round dots punched in to represent the eyes and nose of a conventional human face. The body of the pot was usually kept smooth.

After the pot had been shaped and decorated it was thoroughly dried and baked in hot coals, and entirely covered in order to avoid drafts that might cause damage.

Pots could also have ceremonial functions. They were filled with food for the deceased to use while traveling to the realm of the Great Spirit, and were placed near burial sites.

Pipes

Iroquois men excelled in both the number and the quality of the pipes they made. Early Iroquois clay pipes provided a model for clay pipes used by the whites. Later Iroquois pipes showed a European influence.

Iroquois pipes were of three kinds: elbow, a stone bowl used with separate stems of reed or cane; stalagma, a straight stem attached at right angles to the bowl; and clay, a bowl and stem joined.

Early stone pipes were numerous and beautifully made. The finest pipes, however, were made of clay, with a curved or trumpet-shaped stem and an open bowl in effigy form. The figures on the bowl were representations of human beings, animals, or birds.

Holes in clay pipe stems were usually made with a willow twig, which served as the core and burned away as the pipe was baked. As pipe stems were short, the beaded pipe bag carried by the Iroquois was smaller than that used by the Sioux and other western Indians.

Bark

The Iroquois fashioned many implements and utensils out of elm, hickory, oak, and birch bark, elm bark being the most generally used. Storage barrels, pails, quivers, bowls of all sizes, trays, rattles, troughs for maple sap, traps, canoes, and toboggans were all made of bark. Elm tree sections with the bark left on were used for lining springs where drinking water was drawn, and for lining and covering caches of vegetables and fruits.

Bark was ready to peel when the sap had risen in the elm trees and the leaves were the size of a squirrel's ears. When a large piece of bark was to be removed from a tree, an incision was made through the bark around the tree near the roots, and a similar incision was

Iroquois council pipe.

National Museum of Man
National Museums of Canada
Neg. # 95021

Elm bark dish from the Grand River Iroquois reservation.

National Museum of Man
National Museums of Canada
Neg. # J-3002

made about two meters higher. These two horizontal incisions were then joined by a vertical cut. In order to reach the upper edge of a long strip of bark it was often necessary to build a scaffolding against the tree. Beginning at the edge of the vertical cut, the bark on either side was loosened from the wood with a tapering wedge, which was gradually worked in all around until the large sheet of bark could be easily removed. This thick bark could be divided into thin sheets by peeling it off layer by layer. If bark was removed without injuring the sap layer, the tree continued to grow, and a new layer of bark was formed.

The inner bark of the red elm or black ash was used to make bark barrels. The bark was shaped into a cylinder, with the grain

29

running horizontally. It was overlapped and stitched tightly up the side. A bottom was also stitched on and a lid attached. The barrel was used for storing clothing, dried vegetables, fruits, and seeds. A heavier barrel for grain storage was made from a section of the elm tree by hollowing out an upright, bark-covered log of appropriate length.

A bark sap tub for storing maple syrup was made from a strip of elm bark about sixty centimeters long and ninety centimeters wide. Beginning from where the bark was to be turned up to give it the proper shape, the rough outer bark was removed from both ends, but was left on the bottom and sides. The ends were then turned up and gathered in small folds at the top and tied with a splint or fiber.

To make a bark tray for holding corn meal, mixing corn bread, and other purposes, a strip of bark was prepared by rounding and removing the rough outer surface from the ends, and turning up the ends and sides to form a shallow container. The sides were strengthened by adding splints of hickory both inside and outside of the rim, and stitching over them with bark fibers. Interiors of old bark trays became very smooth with use.

Canoes

The Iroquois made canoes of both red elm bark and oak bark, although the latter was considered more durable. After the rough outer layers had been removed from the large slabs of bark, they were smoothed and soaked, then stitched to a frame of ash or hickory with basswood fiber or splint. Narrow strips of ash serving as ribs were set across the bottom of the canoe, about 30 centimeters apart. The edges of these ribs were turned up and fastened under the

Department of Mines Geological Survey
Neg. # 17129

Dugout canoe on Mackenzie Creek, Iroquois Six Nations Re

Felling a tree by burning and scraping.

rim of the canoe. At each end the canoe was finished with a vertical prow. Iroquois canoes varied in size from 3½ meters (to carry two men) up to 12 meters (with a capacity for thirty men). Bark canoes were extensively used in the fur trade.

The Iroquois also made dugout canoes. Logs were obtained by applying a circle of clay near the base of a tree and starting a fire just below it. When the tree had been burned for a few centimeters, the charred portion was scraped away with a stone chisel. It was often necessary to repeat the process several times before the tree was felled. The log was reduced to the desired length and hollowed out by further charring and scraping.

National Museum of Man
National Museums of Canada
Neg. # J-2998

Iroquois dugout canoe.

Ropes and Tumplines

The Iroquois made thread, twine, and woven burden straps from the fibers of the inner bark of basswood, moosewood or leatherwood, and slippery elm. Indian hemp or Dogbane, nettle fibers, and milkweed fibers were also used in Iroquois weaving. Basswood fiber was especially valuable for weaving rope and the heavier burden belts.

Bark that was to be used for thread was usually gathered in the spring when the sap was running. The outer surface of the bark was removed, then the inner bark was peeled off in narrow strips 2 or 2½ meters in length, loosely braided, and tied in bunches until needed. The bark was boiled and pounded, making it pliable; sometimes it

Use of the tumpline.

was necessary to repeat this process three times. Then it was thoroughly washed and dried in the sun. When dry, the strips of bark were separated into the natural fibers running with the grain. Many of the fibers ran the entire length of the strips of bark and were often one or two meters in length. When separated, the fibers were usually neatly braided into skeins, and saved to be used as thread or twine.

Twine was also used in making fishing nets. In net making, all the strands were held at one end so that they ran lengthwise, then each strand in turn was twisted or knotted with its neighboring strands to make a uniform mesh, producing an open, elastic weave. The work was done with a wooden needle, and was often carried on by the older men of the tribe. Wild hemp was the favorite thread for

Woven tumplines.

National Museum of Man
National Museums of Canada
Neg. # 81493

Use of a tumpline to carry a basket. Photo: F.W. Waugh, 1912.

National Museum of Man
National Museums of Canada
Neg. # 17173

fish nets, but the inner bark of the mulberry, elm, and basswood was also used.

Before the coming of the white settlers, the Iroquois were using bark fibers and Indian hemp to weave or braid long straps, which were used for carrying burdens. The straps were variously known as burden straps, tumplines, pack straps, and carrying straps. The finest quality tumplines were made of slippery elm bark fibers, which were finer, stronger, and more pliable than the basswood fibers used for very heavy tumplines. The fibers were prepared by boiling, stripping, rubbing, and twisting into cords.

The tumpline was usually woven all in one piece, and consisted of a woven belt about 60 centimeters long and 6 centimeters wide with narrow tying strips at each end. In making the belt a twined weave was used; two weft strands of fine fiber were twined over one another between two coarser warp strands. Weaving was begun in the middle of the belt, and narrowed in width near the ends. The remaining length of the warp strands were then braided to form the tie-strings for the packs. On some straps the tying strips were reinforced by braiding strips of tanned deer hide with the fiber. The tie-strings usually extended about 2 meters from each end of the tumpline. The finished tumpline was 4½ meters or more in length, and 8 to 10 centimeters wide.

Though a utilitarian object, the tumpline was often elaborated by the development of geometric designs in the weaving. A ribbed appearance could be obtained by using a finer cross thread. Moose, buffalo, deer, and elk hair was combined with the vegetable fibers to produce patterns. Porcupine quills were also used in the designs. Both hair and quills were dyed to give more color to the burden straps. Rhomboid figures with a narrow white border were often used against an alternate red and blue background. In more recent tumplines, beads were sometimes used in the border.

Some of the finest tumplines had a type of false embroidery, which was worked in during the weaving. Moose hair from between the shoulder and rump of the moose, in its natural white color, or dyed red, blue, and yellow, was wound around the woof threads to form a design.

When in use, the ends of the finished burden strap were attached to the burden basket, cradleboard, or any object that was to be carried on the back. The broad center of the strap was carried across the women's forehead or chest, which bore much of the weight of the burden.

Burden Frames and Cradleboards

The litter basket or burden frame was an article used by the Iroquois to assist in carrying a load. Game, cooking utensils, woodbark, and other small objects could be carried on the frame. The frames were a necessity in every home, and useful in traveling and hunting.

The frame was made of hickory or ash, and was sometimes elaborately carved and finished. The upright part of the frame was longer than the horizontal, and was strung with strips of the inner bark of the basswood. The Iroquois would attach the tumpline to the frame and use the long ties to hold the burden. After being loaded, the frame was placed on the individual's back and the tumpline was passed over the head and carried across the chest.

The cradleboard was used by Iroquois mothers for carrying their babies. The Iroquois made a cradleboard from a flat board about sixty centimeters long and forty-five centimeters wide, with a perpendicular bow near the top and a foot board at the other end, both of which were often elaborately carved. The bow, which was three or more centimeters wide, was braced to stand upright over the board a few centimeters from the top edge, and was held in place by a crosspiece passing under the board into which the ends of the

National Museum of Man
National Museums of Canada
Neg. # 36071, 71645

Two views of a cradleboard: the undecorated top, against which the baby was held, and the heavily decorated bottom.

bow were inserted. Over the bow a blanket, piece of netting, or other covering was drawn to protect the face of the child. A tumpline, attached to the back of the cradleboard, was passed around the forehead of the mother or across the shoulders, so that she could support the baby on her back while traveling. An emergency baby carrier was made of fine twigs compactly woven in much the same form as the cradleboard.

Decorations included inlays of silver and woods of different colors. The backs of cradleboards dating from about 1840 were painted with elaborate floral designs. These highly decorative cradleboards are thought to have been the work of European craftsmen, or of Indians trained by them. They were especially popular among the Mohawk Indians on the St. Regis reservation.

The cradleboard was further elaborated by the addition of a covering, usually of red broadcloth embroidered with beads and decorated with silver ornaments, and with one or more broadcloth bands embroidered with beads. Deer skin strings were run along the outer edges of the board, and, under these, bands to hold the baby in

**Iroquois woman carrying a cradleboard.
Photo: F.W. Waugh, 1912.**

Cradleboard
carried by
a tumpline.

National Museum of Man
National Museums of Canada
Neg. # 17128

place were passed across the body of the child. Rattles were often hung from the bow of the cradle.

Baby hammocks were often made with a rope and a blanket. The rope was stretched between two points up to 2½ meters apart and back again. The blanket was folded so that is was the proper length for the baby's body and three times the desired width. The center of the blanket was then passed under the ropes in such a way that one-third of the blanket could be folded over the ropes from each side to the other, giving three thicknesses to the hammock bottom. Usually two sticks, slightly shorter than the desired width of the hammock, were placed between the ropes at each end of the blanket.

Wooden Utensils

Wooden objects, both plain and carved, were used by the Iroquois in their domestic lives and in their religious ceremonies. Before the introduction of metal tools from Europe, it had been necessary to char the wood and scrape off the burned sections with stone or shell tools in order to produce the desired form. Woodwork became easier when metal tools were introduced in the seventeenth century, and reached the height of its popularity in the eighteenth and early nineteenth centuries.

Iroquois men were noted for their skill in wood carving. Wooden utensils were decorated with figures of animals, birds, and reptiles, usually depicting clan designs and personal totems. Designs representing human figures were also used to a great extent by the Iroquois.

Bowls were made of beech, basswood, and maple. Soft curly maple knots were hollowed out with bone, shell, or stone tools and given a high polish by continual scouring and absorption of grease, which produced an attractive luster. Smaller wooden dishes and spoons were made for children.

Cups of hard maple or other wood were made for individual use by Indians in the northern woodlands. The base was rounded, rather than flat, as the cup was always set on the ground where a small hollow could be made. An animal figure or a design was often carved on the handle of the cup. Warriors tied cups to their belts when traveling.

Wooden mortars for pounding corn were made from the trunk of an oak or other hardwood tree, which was cut to an appropriate length and placed upright. The top was hollowed out with fire, and the charred portion scraped away with a stone chisel. The mortar was usually about 60 centimeters high and 50 centimeters in diameter, and had a symmetrical cavity at one end about 30 centimeters deep. A double-ended pestle of hard maple, about 120

Cayuga Indians using corn mortar.

National Museum of Man
National Museums of Canada
Neg. # 17168

Carved wooden ladles, spoons, and digging stick (right).

National Museum of Man
National Museums of Canada
Neg. # 30810, 30812, 30821

centimeters in length, was made to be held with both hands midway on the handle. Two or three pestles were sometimes used in one mortar when pounding. A smaller mortar and pestle of wood was used to crush sunflower seeds, whose oil was used for food, on hair, and for annointing the false faces used in ceremonies.

Spoons and stirring ladles used for every day and for ceremonial purposes were carved out of cherry, hard maple, white ash, apple, and horse chestnut tree wood. The handles were usually shaped to fit over the edge of a bowl or kettle so that the spoon would not slip in. Ducks, pigeons, and sleeping swans were favorite decorations for handle ends. The bear and dog were also popular subjects for carved objects. After being carved, the spoons were boiled in an infusion of hemlock bark or roots to produce a dark color.

Carving on ladles or paddles made for stirring ceremonial meals often included clan animals in the design. An open-work pattern with a ball inside was carved on some of the handles. These ladles were used in stirring the strawberries at the Strawberry Festival, and the corn soup at the Green Corn Festival.

Basketry

The Iroquois made a great variety of baskets to serve a number of purposes. Baskets made by the various groups and individuals show some minor differences, but certain fundamental techniques were common to basket makers of all six tribes.

The simply woven Iroquois baskets were made to serve a utilitarian purpose, and were not nearly as intricate as the baskets of the far western tribes. Iroquois women were the basket makers, but the men helped in the preliminary heavy work of preparing splints and carving handles. In a few cases the men excelled as basket weavers.

Black ash splints and elm bark were used in Iroquois basket making. Corn husks and flags, or cattails, were also made into baskets by braiding, twining, and plaiting. Sweet grass was made into baskets by coiling.

Black ash splints were plaited in checkered, wicker, twilled, or diagonal and hexagonal styles to make heavy pack, utility, and storage baskets and hampers. These were made both with and without handles and covers. Thin splints of this wood were obtained by hammering a small ash log to loosen the annual layers, pulling these off in thin sheets, and cutting them into narrow strips of even width. Some of the splints were dyed before being used to add color to the baskets.

The Iroquois had several different basket making techniques. Checkered plaiting was a simple over-one-under-one weave using

National Museum of Man
National Museums of Canada
Neg. #50816, 18832

Container made from corn husks.

Pounding out splints for use in basketry. Photo: F.W. Waugh, 1912.

41

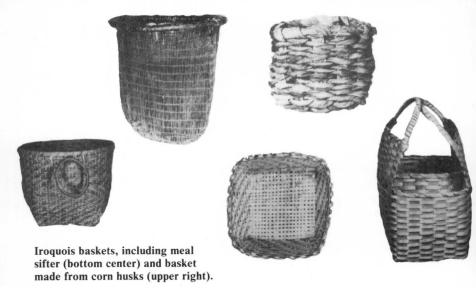

Iroquois baskets, including meal sifter (bottom center) and basket made from corn husks (upper right).

two similar materials that sometimes varied in width. Wicker plaiting was done with a more or less rigid warp and a flexible weft using the same weave.

Diagonal or twilled plaiting used the simple over-and-under weave, but the weft was carried over and under two warps. In each row the plaiting began one strand in advance of the plaiting in the previous row, producing a diagonal pattern in the weave.

Hexagonal plaiting was used in making trays and shallow baskets. It was done with three elements arranged to form an equilateral triangle. The splints in each set went over and under each splint alternately. The members of one element all passed over the members of the second, and under all members of the third group of elements.

A hulling or washing basket about forty-five centimeters deep and forty-five centimeters across the top was made with twilled plaiting. The sides were tightly woven and the bottom formed with an open sievelike weave. It was made both with and without handles. Two open spaces were sometimes left in the weave near the top on opposite sides to provide places in which to insert the hands to carry the basket. On other baskets, raised loops and bail handles were provided.

A shallow sifting basket used in the preparation of corn meal, and for sifting ashes and hominy, was made of hickory splints with a twilled, open plaiting. Shallow rectangular baskets, thirty-three by sixty-six centimeters, were made for drying berries and to serve as bread bowls. A deep basket with flexible sides was made for use as a washing basket.

42

Basket making was stimulated by the white trade as a demand arose for containers to serve an increased number of purposes. Bottle-shaped baskets, women's sewing baskets, laundry hampers, cake baskets with lids, and other baskets that could be used in the homes of settlers were in demand. As late as 1875, baskets were being made in considerable quantities on the St. Regis reservation to be sold among the neighboring white people.

About 1860 a variation in women's work-baskets was achieved by twisting selected splints at regular intervals as plaiting progressed to produce a series of sharp pointed rolls or curls. Because of these projecting curls, this technique came to be known by the descriptive term "porcupine work," although porcupine quills were not used in making these baskets.

Among the implements used by the Iroquois in basket making was a splint cutter. This instrument consisted of a piece of metal with several points, equidistant from one another, inserted in a wooden handle, which was frequently carved. The sharp metal points of the splint cutter, when run down the length of a thin sheet of wood, cut it into splints of equal width for use in basket making.

Putting the final touches to a basket. Photo: F.W. Waugh, 1912.

National Museums of Canada
Neg. # 18851

43

National Museum of Man
National Museums of Canada

Baskets made from ash splints from the Grand River Iroquois reservation.

Carrying baskets, woven with wicker plaiting, were used in gathering corn and firewood, and for carrying provisions and small children. When corn was being gathered, the basket was attached to a tumpline, which was passed around the head or the chest of the worker. The ears of corn were thrown over the shoulder into the basket as they were picked.

A deep basket with an open weave was made for use in fishing. Planting baskets were made with compartments for different seeds, and were tied to the waist, leaving the hands free.

Designs were worked in the black ash baskets by varying the width and color of the splints, by varying the weave, and by giving the baskets different shapes. The splints were colored with vegetable dyes or painted before using.

The Oneidas, who excelled in splint basketry, made a basket of black ash splints in two widths, using checkered plaiting and decorating the side splints on the sides with a border of dots or a geometric or leaf design. The design was applied with paint or by block printing with a potato stamp. Soft red, blue, and yellow colors were used in these designs.

Potato stamps were made by cutting a potato in half and producing a design in relief on the flat surface by cutting away the background. The stamp was then dipped in dye and applied to the wider splints in the basket.

Collections of Iroquois baskets sometimes include miniatures the size of a thimble, made of the root of the gold thread plant. Toy baskets were also carved from peach and plum stones. In addition to the small baskets, small bowls, miniature masks, and dolls were used as charms, or as toys by children.

Snowshoes

Snowshoes were used both while hunting and in warfare, and were necessary for almost one-third of the year. They were built on a light frame of hickory with two or more bracing crosspieces (the toe bar and heel bar) to determine the spread, and were filled in with a web or netting of sinew or skin thongs. They were usually nearly three times as long as they were wide—approximately a meter long and forty centimeters wide—with a rounded, square, or pointed toe. One characteristic of the Iroquois snowshoe was that the space within the toe was usually left without netting for walking in soft snow.

After the men had prepared the frame of the snowshoe, it was filled with a hexagonal web of moose or deer skin rawhide thongs. Three sets of parallel strands were made to cross each other at an angle of 120 degrees, with the result that the meshes were hexagonal in shape. One set of parallel strands was strung diagonally across the middle of the frame, the wrappings going around the frame and bars. Another set of parallel strands, running diagonally in the opposite direction, was strung in the same way. The third set of strands was then laced in with a needle, crossing the intersections of the two previous sets. The needle was a piece of hardwood six centimeters long with pointed ends and a hole in the center.

Thongs of rawhide (babiche) were attached to the center crosspiece of the frame, and were passed around the heel of the wearer to fasten the snowshoe to the foot. The heel was left free to move up and down, and a small opening below the crosspiece allowed the toe of the foot to descend below the surface of the snowshoe as the heel was raised while walking. Women wore a shorter, rounder snowshoe, with the netting extending throughout the frame.

An emergency snowshoe was constructed by bending a long twig into shape and filling it with a netting of vegetable fibers.

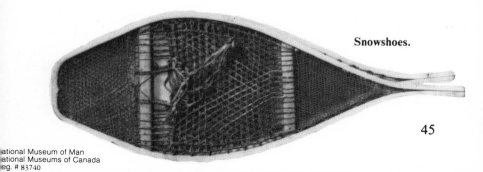

Snowshoes.

ational Museum of Man
ational Museums of Canada
eg. # 83740

Strings of corn. Photo: F.W. Waugh, 1912.

National Museum of Man
National Museums of Canada
Neg. # 23914

Corn Husk and Cob Products

At harvest time when the corn was gathered, the Iroquois women sat in groups in the fields to prepare the ears for storage. Husks were turned back and braided firmly, forming a long rope from which the ears dangled. The braids were hung inside and outside the longhouse while the corn was drying.

Corn husks had many uses: as lamp lighters, kindling, stuffing for pillows, cushions, and mattresses, water sprinklers, cases in which to cook corn pudding, and clotheslines. By braiding, coiling, and sewing, the shredded husks were used to make mats, baskets, moccasins, masks, quivers for arrows, and dolls for ceremonial purposes.

Baskets and pouches of corn husks were tightly woven in various shapes. Watertight salt dishes and bottles were woven of corn husks. Later, bottles and jars were provided with netlike corn husk covers.

Tightly woven corn husk moccasins were made to be used as overshoes. They were oiled and stuffed with buffalo hair for warmth. Braided corn husk ankle bands were worn at dances.

National Museums of Canada
Neg: # 18817

**Sewing corn husk
rounds into mats.**

Corn cobs were used as stoppers for husk salt bottles and for closing the opening in corn husk rattles. Corn cobs served as scrubbing brushes and scratchers. As a fuel, corn cobs were used to smoke meat and hides.

The corn husk sleeping or lounging mat is thought to have been used by the Indians prior to white contact. There are many references to their use in the folklore of the agricultural tribes. The corn husk mat was made up of rows of husks of equal length neatly rolled with the ends folded. The husks for the second row were inserted in the ends of the husks of the first row and tied or stitched in place with basswood cord. The edge of the mat was finished with a tight husk braid. Another type of mat was made from husks that had been loosely braided, coiled, and sewn together with bark thread.

A thick husk door mat was made by braiding strands of the husks in such a way that on one side of the braid the ends were left protruding for a few centimeters. The braid was then coiled to form a round or oval mat, with the rough side on top. The coils were sewn together with corn husk or other fiber. When the mat was finished, the protruding ends of the husks were neatly trimmed to form a short, stiff pile.

Corn husk dolls with hair of corn silk both with and without facial features, were used in certain medicine rites. They were made by folding the husk in a clublike form for the neck and body. The central core was pierced to allow a wisp of husk to be pulled through and braided into arms, and the lower portion was pierced in the same way for the legs. Husks were rolled around the upper portion of the neck to form the head. Husks were then wrapped diagonally across the chest and back to produce the body and shoulders. The legs were braided or neatly rolled into shape, wound spirally with twine, and tied tightly at the ankles. The foot was then bent forward at right angles to the leg and wound into shape. The arms underwent a similar process, but no attempt was made to simulate hands. To cover the head, wide husks were held upward against the top of the head and a string passed loosely around them, and then bent downward, where the string was tightened. This left a little circular opening at the top of the head. The head-cover husks were drawn tightly over the form and tied at the neck, which was afterward wound neatly with a smooth husk. More diagonal pieces were placed over the shoulders and drawn tightly down to the waist. A wide band was then drawn around the waist and tied.

The doll was then ready to have corn silk hair sewn on and its face painted. Dolls were sometimes dressed in husk clothing, but more often cloth or skin was used. They were dressed as warriors or women, and given accessories such as bows, tomahawks, cradle-boards, and paddles.

The corn husk doll was from fifteen to twenty-five centimeters in height, as determined by the length of the corn husk. Small corn husk dolls, about ten centimeters in length, made in response to a dream, were thrown out in the hope that an illness would be discarded as well.

Corn husk doll.

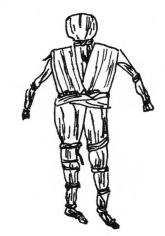

Early 18th Century eleven-strand wampum belt.

National Museum of Man
National Museums of Canada
Slide #   S75-623

Early 19th Century Seneca moccasins decorated with porcupine quill appliqué, blue silk ribbon and white seed beads.

National Museum of Man
National Museums of Canada
Slide #   S75-606

Late 18th Century Mohawk knife and sheath. Sheath is decorated with beads, quills and metal cones. Knife handle is wrapped in tanned skin decorated with quills.

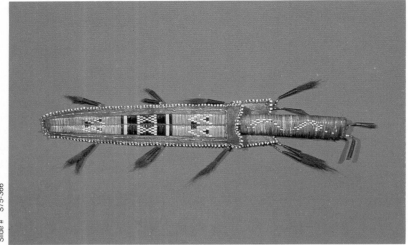

National Museum of Man
National Museums of Canada
Slide # S75-366

Decorated peace pipe.

Mohawk knife sheath decorated with quills, beads and metal cones filled with tufts of dyed hair.

National Museum of Man
National Museums of Canada
Slide #   S75-367

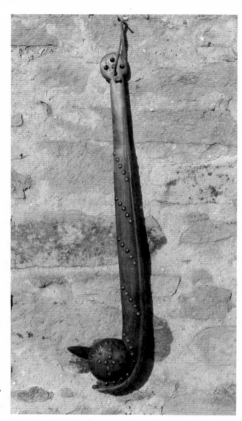

Eastern woodlands war club.

Beaded Iroquois pouch.
Photo: Dr. Frank Lamb

Beaded moccasins.

Woven belt.

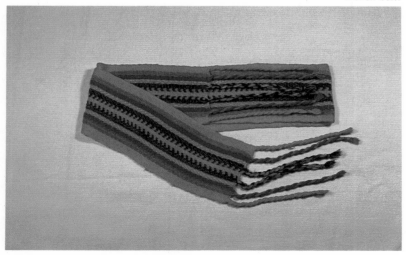

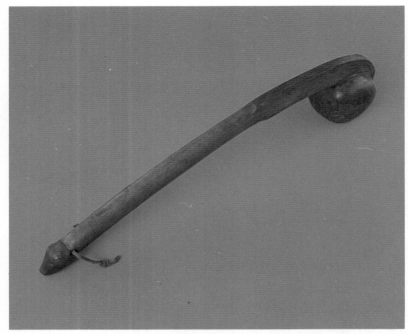

18th Century wooden ball-headed club. The handle end is carved into an animal head, into which glass beads have been inlaid as eyes.

National Museum of Man
National Museums of Canada
Slide #   S75-388

Seneca tomahawk—also a functioning pipe. Blade and bowl are of iron, with wooden handle. c.1800.

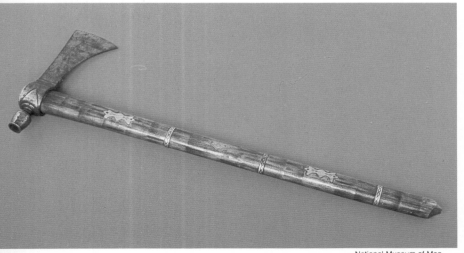

National Museum of Man
National Museums of Canada
Slide #   S75-598

Embroidered moccasins.

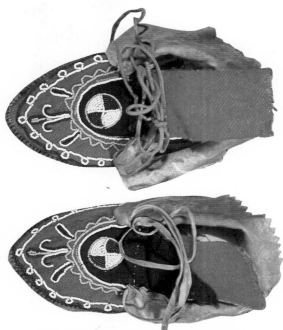

Embroidered moccasins.

Beaded moccasins.

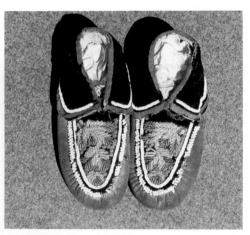

Two carved, wooden cradle boards showing intricate decoration.

Photo: Dr. Frank Lamb

Two Iroquois wooden
false face masks, with
metal circles decorat-
ing the eyes.

Four Iroquois "twisted face" masks—used by the False Face Society.

59

Fine cap of beaded velvet.

Beaded leggings.

60

Two splint baskets—decorated with a black stamp design. A potato was possibly used as the block in making these designs.

This basket's block stamp designs are probably more vivid as a result of subsequent color retouching.

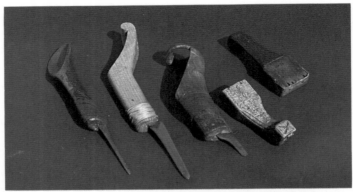

Eastern Indian splint basketry tools—draw knives and gauges for splitting splints into consistent widths.

Two sides of a birch bark basket showing incised designs.

Splint basket from southern Ontario incorporating twisted weft for loop design.

Birch bark and sweetgrass trinket basket.

Colored splint wool basket. The more contemporary elements of plastic and string rope replace the traditional sweetgrass design elements.

Mohawk strawberry sewing basket from St. Regis, N.Y. Curlique twist is used in the splint to create this design.

Sturdy white ash splint baskets.

Weft twist
loop design basket.

A splint basket where warp and
weft splints are completely
covered by either flat or twisted
sweetgrass—creating two
different textures.

Contemporary white ash splint
basket with dyed and twisted
elements used for design. From
the Coughnawauga reserve.

A dried apple face was used on a corn husk doll to represent "Loose Feet," a spirit that granted wishes to little children. To make an apple face doll, an apple that was slightly green was peeled and cored. On one side it was gently molded by hand to produce features, and then hung up to dry slowly. Each day as the apple dried, the features were further molded until they finally resembled a miniature face. A small block of wood was carved for the neck and shoulders, above which was left a piece big enough to fit in where the core had been removed. This supported the head and provided a means of connecting it to the body of the doll.

Tanned Hides

By tanning, a deer hide could be converted into a soft skin that was comfortable for robes and moccasins. It offered a good foundation for the embroidered quillwork at which the women excelled.

A chert blade was used in skinning the deer. Before the skin was tanned, it was hung over a beam while fresh and the hair and grain of the skin were removed with a wooden blade or stone scraper. After scraping, softened deer brains were spread on the skin. If it was necessary to keep the brains for some time before use, they were beaten up into a solution with moss. This gave the mixture enough body to be made into cakes, which were dried by the fire and kept until needed, sometimes for years. The brains of other animals, the spinal cord of an eel, or a mixture of eggs, corn meal, and water or young corn beaten to a pulp was occasionally substituted for the brain mixture in tanning. If a cake of the dried brain mixture was used, it was softened in boiling water, and the moss, used only for preservation, was removed. The skin was soaked in solution for several hours, after which it was wrung out and stretched until it became soft and pliable. If the skin was very thick it might be necessary to soak it several times, so that it would become thoroughly penetrated by the solution.

A fire was then built and the skin hung above it. Each side of the skin was smoked until the pores closed, and the skin had become thoroughly toughened and had turned light brown. The finished skins were used for clothing, other personal articles, and for blankets or robes. The latter were popular with the white settlers as well as the Indians.

Dehairing a deer skin. Photo: F.W. Waugh, 1915.

National Museum of Man
National Museums of Canada
Neg # 34729

Bear skins were dressed with the fur left on. They were first softened in a little clear water, then spread on a log so that the inner surface could be scraped to remove all flesh particles. The clean surface was then thoroughly rubbed with brains or the mixture of eggs, corn meal, and water. Great care was taken not to wet the fur side. When the skin was nearly dry it was worked back and forth until soft over the smooth rounded top of a stake driven into the ground.

Bear skin was used as an article of clothing, as a sleeping robe or mattress, or as a curtain at the opening to the longhouse.

Dyes and Their Preparation

Old pieces of colored quillwork indicate that the Iroquois knew of many natural dyes, but that they began to make use of commercial dyes as soon as they were available. The soft colors of the native dyes were replaced by the brighter aniline dyes.

Skins were sometimes dyed black. However, the Iroquois chose more delicate shades in their quill embroidery work. Dyes from walnut hulls and reddish brown onion skins were used in Iroquois basketry.

The preparation and use of dye in artwork was carried out for the most part by the women. Porcupine quills, elk hair, ash splints, vegetable fibers, and leather were among the materials dyed. Dyes were also used to darken wooden spoons and other wooden utensils. To prepare a dye for wooden spoons, hemlock bark or roots were boiled in water until the liquid was a dark red shade. The spoon was then plunged in and boiled until it had become thoroughly saturated with the dye and had acquired the desired color. With use and time the spoon became almost as dark as ebony and took on a high polish.

Several natural colors were used by the Iroquois, made from various materials. Butternut husks or shucks produced brown. When the butternut husks or the bark of the alder or maple was mixed in solution with sulphate of iron, the dye became black. The shuck of the butternut produced a brownish black, alder bark a purplish black, and maple bark a bluish black.

Yellow was obtained from the seeds of the sweet gale. The seeds were pounded, mixed in water, and boiled for about fifteen minutes. The material to be dyed was added and the boiling continued for another fifteen minutes. The material was then removed from the dye and washed, first in soap and water, then in pure water. It was then wrapped in flannel and dried. The pure yellow that resulted was pale, but very durable.

Blue dye was extracted from green baize by boiling it in water. When the water was deep blue in color, the material was introduced, together with a little powdered alum. Boiling resumed for fifteen minutes, after which the material was removed and washed in pure water. It was essential that the baize be old and worn, as then it retained its yellow and parted with its blue more easily while being boiled. Green could be obtained by boiling a previously dyed yellow article in a blue solution.

Red dye was extracted from the galium root. Sumac seeds, with their pericarp and stalks, were washed in cold water to clean them. They were then boiled in soft water until the water turned a deep, brownish red, after which it was strained through flannel. The pulverized root of the galium was infused in the sumac water, and the material to be dyed was introduced. The temperature was gradually raised to the boiling point, and kept there for several minutes. The material was taken out and rinsed in soft water, then soaked for a short time in a weak soap and water solution. Then it was washed in pure warm water, wrapped up in flannel, and dried.

CLOTHING AND ACCESSORIES

Clothing worn by the early Iroquois in cold weather consisted of furs and tanned skins worn as robes. These were gradually replaced by manufactured materials introduced by the early travelers and traders, but buckskin clothing for working and hunting continued in use up to the nineteenth century. There is evidence that broadcloth was brought in by the English and the French as early as 1537. After Champlain's expedition in 1609, cloth was more generally available.

By the last quarter of the seventeenth century, broadcloth and calico had become popular for both men's and women's garments. Graves of that period indicate that considerable use was made of broadcloth, which was preserved wherever it came into contact with brass or copper kettles in burial sites. In some cases the color as well as the texture has been retained. Silk had come into use by the latter part of the eighteenth century, and velveteen became popular during the last quarter of the nineteenth century. Both silk and velvet were used in decorating broadcloth garments, which had

Iroquois family wearing European-style clothing. Photo: F.W. Waugh, 1918.

National Museum of Man
National Museums of Canada
Neg. # 42726

been the accepted dress of the more prosperous Iroquois since the beginning of the nineteenth century.

The style of these early cloth garments was similar to that of the skin clothing, but gradually both skin and broadcloth clothes were cut after European fashions. Native decorations continued in use—pants, jackets, and vests were trimmed with quills, beads, and fringe.

That the Iroquois prized commercial textiles is indicated by a treaty signed November 11, 1794, in which the United States Federal Government was to make a yearly payment of goods to the Six Nations. Each Seneca was entitled to receive 6 yards (5.6 meters) of calico or 12 yards (10.8 meters) or unbleached sheeting once a year.

Women's Clothing

In early times, an Iroquois woman wore a buckskin wrapper around her body like a skirt, which overlapped from the left side to the right. At the top, the buckskin skirt was folded down a few centimeters over a band of buckskin that was tied around the waist. The overlapping skirt could be thrown back to bare the right leg, allowing the thigh to be used as a working area where strips of

Typical woman's costume of the early 1900s.

National Museum of Man
National Museums of Canada
Neg. # 42724

Iroquois women in skirts and over-dresses. Photo: F.W. Waugh, 1918.

National Museum of Man
National Museums of Canada
Neg. # 42725

buckskin or vegetable fiber could be rolled, a major chore of the women.

Other garments were gradually added to the short buckskin skirt, including leggings, moccasins, and a deer or bear skin robe, dressed with the hair. The robe was finished with a fringe around the armholes and along the lower edge of the skirt. In summer the women continued to wear only the short skirt of skin.

The costume worn by the women in the latter part of the eighteenth century consisted of a skirt of broadcloth or calico (also called turkey cloth) patterned after the old buckskin skirt, a long jacket, an over-blouse or tunic with sleeves, a flannel underskirt, leggings that came only to the knees, and a shawl usually of dark blue broadcloth, about two meters square, which served as a robe or wrap in winter. A small shawl about one meter square was used as a head covering. The shawls were often embroidered in one corner. Broadcloth was preferred by those who could afford it.

Like the early buckskin skirt, the cloth skirt was left open to the knee on the right side. The entire border and the corner on the left side were embroidered with beads or silk ribbon, two decorative elements which were often used in combination.

Skirt border designs usually consisted of the sky dome symbol and the celestial tree, which grew from the top of the sky, and whose curving branches symbolized life. The corner design showed the "big tree of light" that was thought to have existed in the middle of the earth.

The jacket or over-dress showed unmistakable evidence of white contact. Usually of light flannel or calico of solid green, red, or blue, it was made to be loose fitting. Partially gathered at the waist and extending halfway to the knees, it had long full sleeves, a ruffled yoke, and was fastened up the front with silver brooches. Both the jacket and the ruffled yoke were usually finished with a narrow edging of white beadwork, which was often combined with silk ribbon of contrasting color. The clothes of those with wealth and rank were decorated with several rows of silver brooches.

Women's leggings were made of bright red or dark blue broadcloth, slit up the front from ten to fifteen centimeters, ornamented with a narrow border of white beading and colored ribbon along the slit edge, and a wider border across the bottom. A narrow bead edging finished the outer seam. The earlier legging was of deer skin embroidered with porcupine quillwork.

Armlets, knee bands, and waist bands of cloth or velvet decorated with beaded designs formed part of the ceremonial costume. Silver armlets, rings, hair ornaments, and earrings were also used. A beaded scotch cap was worn by the Tuscarora and Seneca women. Beaded bags were carried when wearing broadcloth and velvet costumes. During the early days Mohawk women wore a little sack of seed corn attached to the belt, but this accessory disappeared with the buckskin skirt. After 1860, the majority of Iroquois women had adopted the costume of their white neighbors. Traditionally patterned cloth garments were worn only at festivals.

Hair and skin, as well as clothing, were important to the appearance of the Iroquois woman. Hair was parted in the middle. Married women wore a single braid, doubled up and tied or bound with a quilled or beaded buckskin binder (at one time, an elaborate bone comb). Unmarried women wore two braids and colored the scalp at the part. The hair was well oiled with sunflower oil or bear grease. A red face powder, with a delicate fragrance, made from the pulverized dry-rot of the inner portion of the pine, gave a smooth, velvety finish to the skin.

Men's Clothing

When the first explorers reached North America, the Iroquois man was using animal skin as the main source of his dress. The typical costume consisted of a breechcloth, a fur robe of bear or deer skin made of two skins joined at the upper corners, worn one in front and one at the back, tight deer skin leggings that went above the knees, moccasins, and a turban or skull cap. The skin clothing was often accented by dyed hair and feathers on the headdress, or ermine fringes on the sleeves and the front of the coat. Accessories included knee bands, wrist bands, arm bands, necklaces of bear claws, leg ornaments of deer hoofs, knee rattles, and ornamental belts embroidered with porcupine quills. A utilitarian belt of deer skin, to which necessary possessions could be attached, was wound twice around the waist and tied in front. The war club and scalping knife were worn in the front of the belt by warriors. Face and body painting and tattooing further complemented the costume.

The chief wore a deer skin belt over one shoulder, diagonally across the chest, and tied at the left side. Both this belt and his waist belt were decorated with porcupine quills in woven or embroidered patterns. On ceremonial occasions the deer skin shoulder belt was

Iroquois man wearing fringed leather leggings. Photo: C.M. Barbeau, 1949.

National Museum of Man
National Museums of Canada
Neg. # J-3138

replaced by a sash woven of natural fibers or of brightly colored yarn with a long fringe at the ends. This sash was the most prized article of the costume.

The early leggings of tight fitting deer skin came up to the thigh and had strips or thongs of skin to attach them to the belt worn around the waist. They extended to the moccasins and were fastened at the knees with garters. The leggings were decorated up the front with porcupine quill embroidery. While those worn by warriors were fringed at the outer seam, those worn in times of peace were not fringed. Leather leggings and moccasins were worn to some extent until the middle of the nineteenth century.

The later leggings were of red or dark blue broadcloth cut on straight lines, and were broad and loose fitting. The broadcloth legging was finished with a wide band of beading across the bottom and a beaded border along the seam up the front of the leg.

The Iroquois were influenced early in the colonial period by European dress. They began to wear leather hunting coats and pants cut in European fashion. Leather pants or leggings were

National Museum of Man
National Museums of Canada
Neg. #J-3137

Boy in traditional Iroquois costume. Photo: C.M. Barbeau, 1949.

Bureau of American Ethnology, 21st Annual Report, 1899-1900

Cayuga chief wearing sash.

73

sometimes fringed and decorated with porcupine quills and beads, and brass buttons were used on the leather coats. White shirts that hung outside the trousers were a later addition to men's clothing. Elaborate Iroquois costumes were prepared for use in dances. The shirt fronts or vests worn at ceremonies were often heavily beaded with floral designs.

At one time the men wore a fringed kilt of softly tanned doe skin. It was fastened around the waist by a belt and hung to the knees. Quillwork and ornaments were used for decorating the kilt, which was a favorite article of dance clothing. In later years various fabrics were substituted for deer skin in making the kilt.

The breechcloth of deer skin or broadcloth was approximately a quarter of a meter wide and two meters long. It was passed between the legs and drawn up through the belt at the front and back so that the ends hung down over the belt in front and behind. Designs were often beaded on one or both ends of the breechcloth.

Until the middle of the nineteenth century, most of the men wore long hair divided into two braids. However, during times of war, warriors shaved or burned their hair, leaving only a scalp lock.

Warriors required special protection for the head from the

Iroquois man in traditional leggings and white shirt.

Alec General, Iroquois Chief. Photo: C.M. Barbeau, 1949.

National Museum of Man
National Museums of Canada
Neg. # 34706

National Museum of Man
National Museums of Canada
Neg. # 1-3136

stroke of a war club. In the early days the head or skin of a raccoon or other small animal was used as a head covering. Greater protection was achieved by the development of a round cap woven of willow sticks in two layers. Later this type of helmet was made over a frame consisting of a band of splints shaped to fit the head like a skull cap or turban, with two cross splints arched over the top.

The cap not only protected the head but also was used for adornment. It was covered with tanned skin, red or blue broadcloth, velvet, or a fancy silk handkerchief, and fastened at the rim with a quilled, beaded, or silver band. A cluster of soft feathers was attached to the top of the cap with a single long eagle plume set in the tip of the crown, arching backward. The eagle feather, which was the distinctive feature of the cap, was loosely set so that it twirled or quivered with every motion of the wearer or with the slightest breeze. On the warpath, the men wore a headpiece like that of the Ojibwa, made of deer tail hair.

In the early part of the nineteenth century, the men and even some of the women wore the tall beaver or "plug" hats then fashionable among the whites. On the tall crown of the hat they placed band after band of silver, according to their wealth.

A necklace of sweet grass, worn with the traditional costume by both sexes, was made up of fragrant marsh grass, and braided into three-strand cords. Every eight or ten centimeters it was decorated with small disks of sweet grass. These were sometimes ornamented with beadwork in simple designs. The disks resembled the old stone runtees—round ornaments also made of shell. Fourteen of them were customarily used on a neck piece.

Moccasins

Iroquois footwear consisted of soft-soled moccasins sewn with sinew thread and a "moccasin needle," which was a small bone that was taken from near the ankle joint of a deer. One variation of the moccasin was that of the Cayuga and the Seneca, which was made of one piece of skin with the seam at the heel and over the top of the foot, leaving the bottom seamless. At the back, half a centimeter overlapped on each side, giving added strength to the seam. The seam up the front of the moccasin was gathered, with notches cut out between the gathers so that the two sides could be pulled tightly together. After the seam had been made, the gathers were beaten or

Iroquois moccasins.

National Museum of Man
National Museums of Canada
Neg. # 36058, 83740

pounded so that they would lie flat. The gathered seam was often covered with a narrow strip of quillwork or beadwork. In some cases fine beadwork was done directly on the moccasin at the sides of the seam.

The Mohawk in the eastern part of New York made a different type of moccasin, similar to that of the Algonquian, in which the toe was gathered into a U-shaped vamp that was sometimes decorated. In some cases, a separate piece of the same shape as the vamp was elaborately embroidered with quills or beads, and tacked over it. These decorative vamps were removed from worn moccasins and used again on new ones.

The Iroquois moccasin extended several centimeters above the ankle and was fastened with deer skin thongs drawn through holes on each side. Usually the top of the moccasin was turned down to form a cuff. In the moccasin worn by women, this cuff was a single piece. In the men's moccasin, the cuff was separated at the back seam so that the two sides spread apart.

The cuffs of Iroquois moccasins were decorated at different periods with embroidery of moose hair bristles, woven and embroidered porcupine quillwork, bead embroidery, or ribbon-work, as the different materials became available. A pair of old Seneca moccasins shows porcupine quills, fine beads, and silk ribbonwork all used together. Small metal disks and cotton and silk braids were used with bead designs in moccasin decoration. The cuffs of early moccasins were sometimes finished by fringing the edge of the skin, by adding a fringe of moose hair bristles, or with a plaited quill border.

Velvet and broadcloth cuffs were popular on later moccasins. Both black and brown velvet, and red and black flannel were used for cuffs. The edges of velvet cuffs were bound with cotton cloth or cotton braid, or with silk ribbon. An old pair of Tuscarora moccasins shows black velvet cuffs bound in red woolen braid.

Moose hair embroidery on moccasins was worked in delicate scroll and floral patterns. Porcupine quills were used in scrolls, in interlaced zigzags, and in fine floral patterns. Bead embroidery patterns ranged from very fine triangles, scrolls, and double curve designs on the Seneca and Cayuga moccasins to heavy floral designs on the Tuscarora and Mohawk moccasins. Opaque, translucent, and transparent beads in many different sizes were used in moccasin decoration at different periods.

Bags

At different stages of their culture, the Iroquois made bags to suit their various needs. Bags were made of such materials as fur and woven vegetable fiber, and some bags were elaborately beaded with a cloth or tanned skin background. The entire skin (with the head and tail left on) of the white weasel, mink, squirrel, fawn, or marten was made into a bag to serve as a knapsack or tobacco pouch. As a knapsack the bag was filled with food for an expedition, and hung from the girdle of the warrior or hunter. A small tobacco bag or "fire bag" was made for carrying a short-stemmed pipe. Similar bags were in constant use in the home for holding valuables. Bags of tanned skin served as containers for strings of wampum. They were approximately fifteen centimeters deep and twenty centimeters wide, usually slightly narrower at the top, and laced up the sides with a strip of skin. These bags were finished with an eight or ten centimeter flap at the top, and a ten or twelve centimeter fringe at the bottom. Leather strings were provided for carrying. Another type of carrying bag was flat and rectangular in shape, about twenty-three by thirty centimeters, and made of basswood fiber in both close and open weaves.

From the middle of the eighteenth century through the early half of the nineteenth century, white influence showed up in Iroquois bag making. Small, flat beaded bags were made of

Iroquois bags.

National Museum of Man
National Museums of Canada
Neg. # J-3335

commercial cloth, and were modeled after the prevailing style of side bag worn on the belt by white women of the period. They were approximately fifteen by fifteen centimeters and almost hexagonal in shape, but were usually curved across the lower edge and had a flap falling over from the top. Many were decorated with rows of fine beads in several colors. Some of the rows were separated by a beaded zigzag pattern that closely resembled rickrack, while others were embroidered with bead designs in which a double curve pattern was used. Silk ribbon was often inserted between rows of beads for color, and often these elaborately beaded articles were finished with cotton lining and binding. Beaded belts were sometimes made to wear with the bags, much as the white woman wore hers.

Around 1860 a new type of heavily embossed embroidery done with opaque white glass beads appeared on bags and other articles made by the Tuscarora and the Mohawk. The coming of tourists to Niagara created a demand for souvenirs, and the Iroquois responded by making bags, pin cushions, and needle cases in many shapes and heavily embroidered with bird and flag designs. Large translucent beads were among the most popular materials for these articles. Beaded strings ending in metal cones filled with dyed moose hair were sometimes used as a finish around the edge of a bag. Beautiful as some of the articles were, the decoration was often heavy and inappropriate, a fact which rendered them useless for their intended purposes.

Woven Yarn Sashes

The ornamental sashes of the Iroquois were similar to those worn by the French voyageurs in the eighteenth century. Bright-colored European wools were used in making the sashes, which were woven by hand, without loom, heddle, bobbin, or shuttle. Frequently, 140 or more strands were finger woven into the sashes, and about forty strands were used in narrow garters. Two or more of the narrow strips were sometimes stitched together overhand to form a broad sash, twenty-five centimeters or more in width.

The Iroquois, like the western Woodland Indians, enriched the woven sashes by the addition of white beads, which were carried on a special thread, and were woven in so as to outline the zigzag, diamond, and hexagonal designs. The sharp pointed zigzag design suggested lightning and arrow points. V and W designs predominated in the narrow sashes. Beads were also worked into the deep

Bureau of American Ethnology, 21st Annual Report, 1899-1900

Cayuga warrior wearing woven sash and holding tomahawk pipe.

National Museum of Man
National Museums of Canada
Neg. # 74613

Caughnawaga Indian in traditional costume. Photo: C.M. Barbeau, 1930.

yarn fringes (fifty centimeters to one meter in length) at both ends of the sash.

Many of the sashes were made of a single color, usually red. Two shades of blue, sage green, a rich shade of old gold, and white were also used. As many as five colors appear in some sashes. The red sashes, 9 to 12 centimeters wide, sometimes had a border of dark green or another color 1¼ centimeters wide on each side, with white beads woven into the border and body of the sash.

A fine, close weave was sometimes used in making the sashes. With a tightly spun commercial wool this produced a firm texture. Other sashes were loosely woven and soft. Cheap, machine-made imitations of the old sashes were numerous, but they can easily be distinguished from the handmade finger-woven sashes of the Iroquois.

Silver Ornaments

The use of silver by the Iroquois dates from the seventeenth century, when the French and Dutch came into the country with metallic instruments. Silver medals, gorgets, beads, rings, earrings, and other ornaments were popular and were lavishly used among the western Iroquois during the colonial period. They superseded the earlier bone, copper, shell, and polished stone ornaments. Copper and wire bracelets, arm bands, brooches, and earrings; bronze rings; and copper beads were worn up to the middle of the eighteenth century.

Iroquois silversmith making drops for earrings. Photo: F.W. Waugh, 1912.

National Museum of Man
National Museums of Canada
Neg.# 18829

80

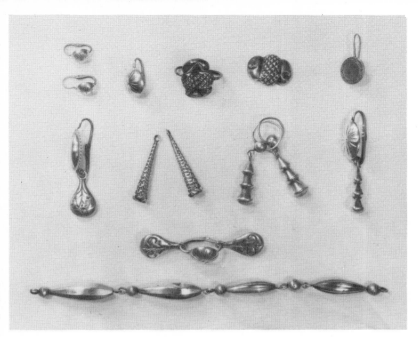

National Museums of Canada
Neg. # 83952

Silver jewelry.

The Iroquois of New York were the leading producers of silver jewelry. Silversmiths in almost every Iroquois village followed a profitable trade, which did not die out until about 1865. Silver medals and coins from land purchases were pounded out on an anvil, cut into patterns with metal punches and chisels, then decorated with incised, embossed, and openwork designs. The many designs included dots, straight lines, curved lines, fine zigzags, tiny triangles, sun, moon, and star symbols, hearts, and diamonds, as well as monograms and heads in full face or profile, which were often used on silver rings and medals. Silver armbands and headbands for both men and women were also made by white silversmiths and sold in large numbers to the Indians.

Crosses became popular after the coming of the Jesuits in 1654, but seem to have been used primarily for ornamental purposes rather than for their religious significance. Many of the crosses were plain, but others had ornamental ends, some of which were decorated with floral designs. Among the larger pieces has been found a double barred cross, which resembles the archiepiscopal, pectoral, or processional cross used in the church at that time.

Brooches were the most numerous of silver ornaments and were used to fasten and decorate the costumes of both men and women. As many as two or three hundred brooches were worn on

81

National Museum of Man
National Museums of Canada
Neg. # 20877

Silver brooches.

one outfit. The brooches were also used to decorate ribbons, headbands, and sashes, and to fasten the wide band of broadcloth used on cradleboards. The number of brooches worn was indicative of the wealth of the wearer.

The brooch itself was a thin silver disk with a central opening across the front of which a silver tongue, loosely attached at one end, extended as on a buckle. The cloth could be pinched up in this central opening and the silver tongue passed through it to hold it in place.

Brooches varied in form, circumference, and in size of aperture. Up to eight centimeters in diameter, they were cut in various artistic forms on which designs were engraved, stamped, or embossed. The form and decoration of the brooches closely resembled silverwork of European origin.

EMBROIDERY
AND BEADWORK

As a result of early contact with white settlers, the traditional decorative artwork of the Iroquois decreased and gave way to the production of articles made of commercial materials using styles borrowed from the Europeans. Skins were replaced by broadcloth, calico, and silk; moose hair and vegetable fibers gave way to commercial yarns in embroidery work; and porcupine quills gradually ceased to be used in decorative patterns as imported glass beads became available. Beads, originally used on skins, were applied to broadcloth, a combination that was popular for many years. Silk was used in appliqué and as a background for bead designs as early as the latter part of the eighteenth century.

Beaded bag, knife sheath, mittens, and leggings.

83

National Museum of Man
National Museums of Canada
Neg. # J-3335, J-4006

Moose Hair Embroidery

Moose hair was used by the Iroquois to embroider designs on tanned skin and birch bark. The hair, which averaged five centimeters in length, came from the mane, cheeks, and rump of the moose. It was fine, dark brown in color at the outer tip, a lighter greenish tan color at the center, and white at the root end. The hair was lighter on winter-killed moose. Moose hair was used because it took dyes well, and it was often colored with soft, natural dyes when used for embroidery.

Because of the fineness of moose hair, several hairs were used together in making embroidery stitches. Very fine stitches were used to fasten them to the tanned hide or bark. In another technique, the hairs were inserted from the outside of the skin or bark, carried through again to the outside, and trimmed off evenly a short distance from the surface, much as a hooked rug is made.

Delicate floral designs were usually created with moose hair, occasionally with a figure of a bird, animal, or person worked in. Floral designs embroidered in moose hair on red broadcloth show strong French influence. Indian girls and women probably became acquainted with French floral designs early in the seventeenth century, when they studied under the nuns in the French convents.

Quillwork

The Iroquois used porcupine quills in their weaving and embroidery. Their early skin robes, moccasins, and quivers were elaborately decorated with quills woven or embroidered in patterns similar to the work of the Northern Algonquian tribes (Ojibwa, Cree, and Ottawa). Quillwork in birch bark was not developed to so great an extent by the Iroquois as among the other Woodland tribes. Only a few examples of this woven quillwork remain.

Fine geometric designs in coordinating colors were developed in the weaving. In embroidery work some delicate floral patterns were worked out with very fine, young quills, but most of the embroidery designs were geometric because of the stiffness of the quills.

In early work, undyed white quills with their brown tips were used effectively in the old tribal designs. Later the quills, sorted according to diameter and length, were dyed a number of colors and kept in cases made from the bladder of an elk or another large animal. Prior to application, quills were soaked for an hour or more in water, and then chewed flat before being embroidered onto the skin with a sharp thorn (later a steel awl), which served as a needle, and sinew thread.

Beadwork

The use of beads as decoration dates back to the pre-contact period. Beads of stone, bone, pottery, and shell have been found at burial sites and in excavations of villages. When the Dutch reached Manhattan in 1609, they found the coastal Algonquian making large quantities of disk shaped (discoidal) and cylindrical beads from small, freshwater, spiral shells. These were pierced through the center, and strung on threads of deer sinew or bark. With their steel instruments, the Dutch soon developed more efficient methods of making beads and other shell ornaments, and sold them to the Indians in great numbers. The Indians later purchased steel drills for their own use, and the native production of shell articles was vastly increased.

Leggings showing intricate vegetal designs.

Cayuga chief in beaded skin shirt and traditional cap with eagle feather.

Neg. # 36065

Bureau of American Ethnology, 21st Annual Report, 1899-1900

Small discoidal, spherical, and cylindrical shell beads have been found in large numbers in sites that were occupied around the middle of the seventeenth century. Beads and ornamental disks or runtees of shell have also been found in graves of the late seventeenth and early eighteenth centuries. The runtees were large ornaments of shell, most of which were decorated with incised or picked-in designs.

Few shell beads have been found on sites dated later than the eighteenth century. After 1800, wampum strings and belts of shell beads were used primarily in councils and for ceremonial purposes. At an early date, European travelers offered commercial glass beads to the Indians in trade. Records show that imported beads were supplied to the Mohawks as early as 1616, and beads have been found in excavations of villages dating from that period. By the eighteenth century, commercial beads were in common use. They had replaced both the quills and the small shell disks that were previously used for ornamental purposes. Commercial thread gradually replaced sinew.

Bead embroidery was used to decorate both skin and cloth by the Iroquois. The old quilled patterns were used in bead embroidery. Beads were attached to the skins with sinew, being couched down by use of the spot stitch just as the quills had been. When the spot stitch was used, two threads were necessary. The beads were strung on one thread that was carried along in the direction desired. It was fastened down by a second thread, which was carried across it after every two or three beads. The threads were pulled tight to hold the beads in place.

The use of thread and needle in the later beadwork on cloth made it possible to work out complicated, curved designs. The elaborate Iroquois bead patterns of later years bear no apparent relation to the earlier, simpler ones done on skins with sinew and awl. Substitution of a new type of decoration apparently took place gradually, for on a few of the old pieces of handwork, the three types of ornamentation are to be found—quillwork, beadwork, and shell decoration.

Beadwork was being carried on in almost every St. Regis home during the last half of the nineteenth century. In many cases it was a hobby, but in others it was carried out as a cottage industry, with hired labor. Fancy articles of great variety were being made of brightly colored cloth embroidered with clear glass beads. Sewing machines were often used to stitch up the seams in the cloth.

Ribbonwork

During the latter part of the eighteenth century, ribbons began to decorate Iroquois clothing. Though they did not develop elaborate ribbonwork patterns like those of the Woodland tribes on the Great Lakes, the Iroquois used ribbons extensively. They were applied as borders, or as a background for the white beads that sometimes decorated their later costumes. Colored ribbon borders were usually finished on both sides with one or more rows of white beads, or were used as a background for beaded scrolls and flowers.

Ribbonwork was used on skin moccasins and on broadcloth costumes. It decorated arm, wrist, and neck bands, and was found on bags and other accessories of both men and women.

Tablecloths, Bedspreads, and Blankets

The Iroquois were quick to apply their skill in decoration to tablecloths, handbags, pincushions, and other articles brought from Europe, using traditional designs. Around 1860, they began to embroider floral designs in colored beads that were arranged to produce a shaded effect, apparently in an attempt to copy European beadwork. This heavy bead embroidery was used by the Tuscarora

Iroquois woman in skirt with heavily decorated border.

National Museum of Man
National Museums of Canada
Neg. # 42716

87

National Museum of Man

Iroquois in traditional costume, including bear claw necklaces. Photo: C.M. Barbeau, 1949.

on round ceremonial caps, bags of various shapes, and velvet moccasin cuffs.

Bedspreads, blankets, and tablecloths, usually of red broadcloth, were decorated with large floral designs in the center, and deep curved borders of beads around the outer edge. These resembled the earlier blankets, which were decorated with moose hair embroidery, but a much heavier design of raised beadwork was used later by the Tuscarora. The scalloped borders were made up of as many as ten rows of line beading in several colors, carried carefully around the curves. These were four centimeters or more in width, and similar to those used on the side bags worn on a lady's belt. The outside edge was sometimes finished with a scalloped loop of white beads, and the inside with white beads grouped in small, effectively spaced pyramids. Fine beads were usually used for these borders.

Border design.

Iroquois border designs in bead and appliqué.

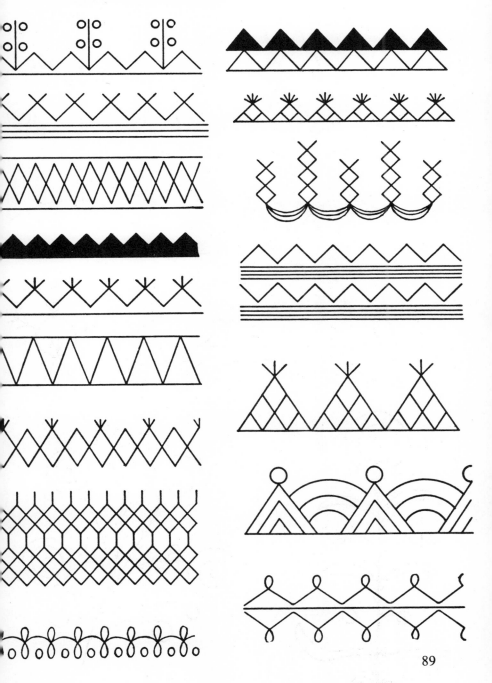

Celestial or World Tree design variations.

Design Symbolism

Symbolism was an integral part of Iroquois design. Although the Iroquois lacked a written language, they used pictographs, wampum belts, wampum strings, and other symbolic designs as memory aids to record contracts and treaties, while tally cards were used for less formal records.

Feast bowls were decorated with beaver tail designs, which symbolized peace and plenty. Design units of the sky dome (half circle), the sun (conventional form), horned trimmings (scroll or helix), the celestial or evergrowing tree (natural or geometric form), and the council fire (hexagon or square), represented celestial, geographical, and mythical phenomena.

The Iroquois nations symbolized peace by a tree whose top they said reached to the sun, and whose branches not only offered shelter and repose, but also extended so far that they could be seen at a great distance. The Iroquois pine tree was an emblem of the confederacy, and was variously known as the "evergrowing tree," the "world tree," the "great earth tree," the "tree of life," the "tree of peace," and the "celestial tree." The Iroquois believed it stood at the center of the world, and bore aloft the sun and moon on its branches. According to other legends it bore luminous blossoms, which provided light for humans. Its great white roots were thought to penetrate to the primal turtle on whose back the earth rested.

Scroll, helix, or tendril designs had various implications. The Tuscarora called them violets, meaning "bowing the head," and regarded them as a sign of good luck. The Mohawk called scroll designs "fern heads" or "horned" trimmings. Scrolls also represented horns of office. Deer antlers were the emblem of chieftainship and high rank. Horns curving outward denoted a living chief, while those curving inward were emblematic of a dead chief. In most cases the curves in the Iroquois designs turned outward rather than inward.

The circle was among the oldest of the designs used in quill embroidery. It was regarded as a symbol of life, its unbroken circumference being symbolic of the continuation of life in the world beyond. On some old buckskin robes the circle was embroidered in red quills, and usually surrounded by a border in radiating lines of lighter colored quills. The red circles or disks were used on the front of the costume, usually one near each shoulder, or on the breechcloth.

Colors, like designs, had symbolic meanings. A sacred red paint was used in ceremonies. White beads were used to express peace, health, and harmony. Dark purple or black beads represented sorrow, death, mourning, or hostility. Red beads were used to make a declaration of war or to offer an invitation to join in making war.

Scroll designs.

92

Border designs using the scroll and sky dome.

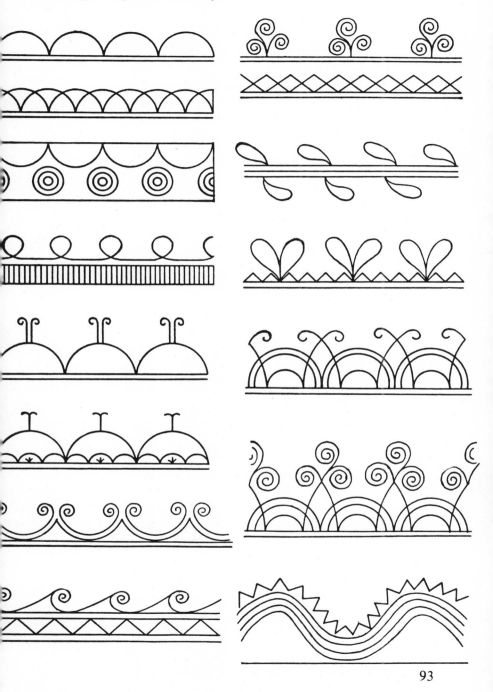

93

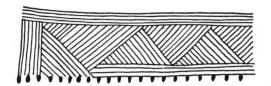

**Portion of border design from
an Iroquois pottery vessel.**

Two quill border designs.

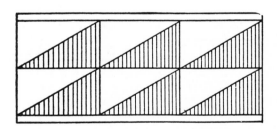

Quill design used on a headband.

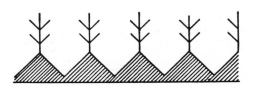

Two quill designs.

Common Designs

The Iroquois used a wide variety of designs developed under widely differing influences, and with different materials. Intertribal contacts, the coming of the colonists, and the introduction of new materials and tools resulted in radical changes in design styles.

The early use of design can be studied on pieces of pottery and on wood carvings collected from old village sites. During the sixteenth and seventeenth centuries the Indians of New York State decorated their pottery with geometric designs, which consisted of groups of parallel, straight lines in angular combinations incised or carved in the clay. For a brief period, beginning in the latter part of the sixteenth century, animal forms were used. The bowls on their clay pipes were modeled with a high degree of realism, human and animal forms being most commonly used. The modeled, rather than carved, type of sculpture found its greatest development among Indians in these Iroquois pipes.

To some extent the designs on wood resemble those on pottery. Wooden utensils were decorated with zigzag and other straight line designs. Geometric designs were followed by the more elaborately carved realistic figures that characterize many of the later Iroquois utensils.

Some of the oldest Iroquois designs are those found on tumplines woven of vegetable fibers. They were geometric and incorporated diagonal lines, rectangles, triangles, and rhomboid shapes, all of which were usually stepped when worked out in the weaving. Similar designs occurred in the wampum and woven yarn belts, as well as zigzag and V- or W-shaped patterns. The otter-tail pattern, popular with the Indians of the Great Lakes, was often used by the Iroquois on woven yarn sashes, where the pattern was worked in white beads.

Early quill designs were largely geometric, due to the stiffness of the quills and the technique used. Zigzag and triangular patterns predominated on the woven or plaited quillwork used as bands and borders. Long scroll designs worked in quills sometimes appeared on the woman's costume. A circle shape was often used as a unit design, and was filled in solidly with quills. Very fine floral designs were used in some of the early quill embroidery work. Similar fine designs were embroidered with moose hair at an early date.

Geometric designs were less prominent in later quill embroidery

Sky dome symbols, done in moose hair and quill embroidery.

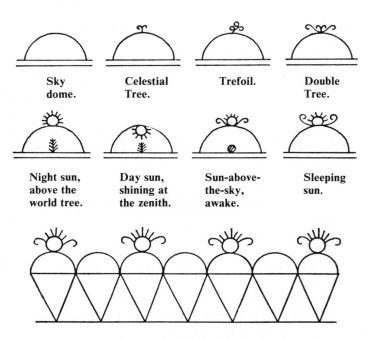

| Sky dome. | Celestial Tree. | Trefoil. | Double Tree. |

| Night sun, above the world tree. | Day sun, shining at the zenith. | Sun-above-the-sky, awake. | Sleeping sun. |

Borders emboidered in moose hair on deerskin garment.

Two-curve pattern.

Sky domes, resting upon the Earth.

Series of trees.

Suns and celestial trees, resting on sky domes.

From *Certain Iroquois Tree Myths and Symbols*
Authur C. Parker.

work. The double curve motif found in early quill embroidery work on leggings, moccasin flaps, skirts, and bags was gradually superseded by floral designs.

The mythological turtle (on which, in legends, the earth was built, having been brought up from a piece of mud), the crane, hawk, heron, bear, wolf, deer, snipe, and beaver were clan figures used as unit designs by the Iroquois. These were pictured as clan figures in embroidered quillwork or beadwork on the skin robe, breechcloth, or other part of the man's costume.

Distinctive Iroquois styles of bead embroidery, usually in patterns common to all five nations, were developed with new materials that were made available through trade. White bead embroidery patterns with scroll motifs used on broadcloth and calico costumes were characteristic of the Iroquois. The designs of the Seneca and the Cayuga are best known and are probably the most distinctive.

Border patterns done in white beads on dark broadcloth are found on leggings, robes, and women's clothing between the mid-eighteenth and nineteenth centuries. Fine white seed beads were usually used in border patterns, though sometimes other types of beads, either larger or of different styles, were used according to their availability through trade. Color could be introduced by running silk ribbon along the edge of the garment under the beads, or by using a piece of colored silk as a background for small beaded diamonds or circles. A floral design known as the "celestial tree," a tree that was supposed to contain every kind of fruit and flower, often decorated one corner of the blanket or skirt. The design, done in delicately colored beads and ribbon, incorporated two harmonizing colors, often light blue and old rose.

A popular unit design consisted of an inverted semicircle resting upon two parallel, horizontal lines. From the top of this two lines curved outward like the end of a split dandelion stalk. The semicircle represented the sky dome, the parallel lines the earth, and the curved lines the celestial tree. In some patterns, the curves occurred in a trefoil, in others as a double tree. Sometimes a sun with radiating rays occurred above the semicircle, with or without the celestial tree. The tree was further elaborated by superimposing various other forms.

Beaded border designs ranged from rows of beads in straight lines or in simple, undulating curves, to elaborately worked lacy patterns in which semicircles and scrolls predominated. The "pot-

Early Seneca costume, showing areas of decoration.

Floral design done
in quills.

Seneca breech cloth designs.

hook" or "scorpion" design was prominent in most of the patterns in which curves were used. The units of these elaborate designs were frequently based on a double curve. A balanced pattern was often repeated along the border. The double curve motif was generally used in the isolated designs found on hair ornaments, bands for baby cradles, moccasin yokes, and knife sheaths.

The line designs used along the edge of the garments were done in parallel rows, sometimes one centimeter or more deep, and occasionally in varied colors. Alternately, short lines were used in groups of three or five, radiating from circles, semicircles, or curved borders. Short lines were also attached at intervals to the stems in floral designs, giving the appearance of thorns. They may have represented either leaves or the sun's rays.

Sometimes a beaded row of small isosceles triangles was used in combination with the parallel lines that made up the border. If embroidered with very fine beads, the triangular designs had a delicate, lacy effect. A deep lattice work, with alternate diamonds partially crossed or stippled, was frequently included in the border design. The lattice design was usually found in combination with the scroll or other curved designs.

Semicircles were frequently used in border patterns to give a well defined scalloped design. More often, semicircles were combined with lattice and radial designs and were embellished with a simple hook design, which was sometimes doubled, or with scrolls used singly, or in groups of two or three. Concentric circles were used to represent both flowers and buds. Beads in two or more colors were often used in alternating rows of concentric circles, with a row of white beads between.

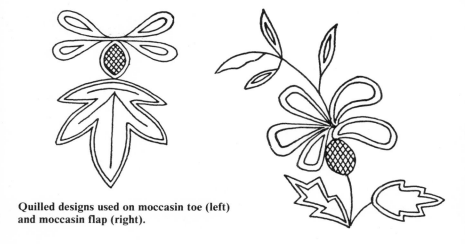

Quilled designs used on moccasin toe (left) and moccasin flap (right).

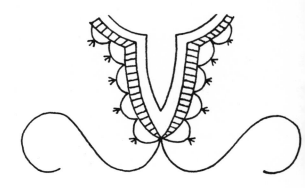

Quill design from
man's tunic.

Design done in white
beads on Seneca
woman's costume.

Quill pattern from
knife sheath.

Design from moccasin yoke.

Border patterns.

Embroidered border patterns of white beads were most often finished with a beaded edging, which took the place of the leather fringe used on earlier garments. Sometimes on less elaborate costumes the beaded edging was used alone without a border pattern. In forming the edge, the beads were arranged so that every other bead stood out at right angles to the beads along the edge of the material, thus giving an attractive finish to the garment. The edge of the garment was sometimes scalloped before being beaded. A large number of beads were used in working out this border pattern to give a deeper edge.

Several different methods were employed to make the beaded edging. In the most commonly used method, thread was passed through a bead, through the edge of the material, and up through the first bead again. Two beads were then added to the thread and the thread was again passed through the material, then again through the two beads. Two more beads were added, and the work continued as before. In the finished edging, the beads were alternately vertical and horizontal, the latter being those attached directly to the edge.

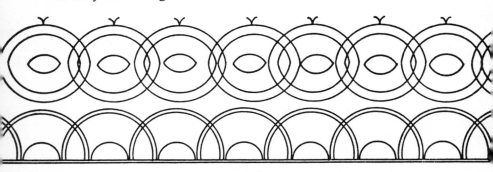

Border designs.

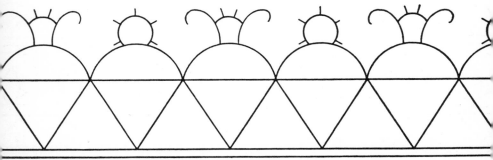

Heavy floral designs, embroidered with the "lazy stitch" in beads of many colors, are found on velvet bags, caps, and moccasin vamps and cuffs. These embroidery designs differ from border designs both in technique and choice of colors. Though they probably arose from different sources, they seem to have been used during the same period (1806-1890). The heavier floral designs were usually made with large beads. Opaque or pearl-colored beads were especially popular. The beads were strung on sinew, which was tacked to the skin by inserting it on the upper surface of the skin after a hole had been made by an awl. So many beads were strung on the sinew that, when the sinew was again fastened to the skin, the beads could not be drawn close, but were left raised in the finished

Beaded floral designs.

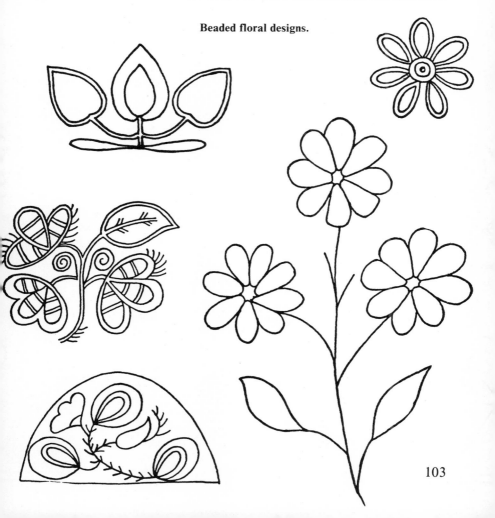

103

embroidery. Sometimes an embossed appearance was achieved by inserting padding underneath.

Navy, light blue, turkey red, and green were popular color choices for clothing. Materials such as calico, broadcloth, flannel, and ribbon of these colors were embroidered, most often with white beads. Colored beads were introduced into some circle and flower designs. Colored silk was used for borders, usually with an edging of white beads. Old rose silk was often used with white beads.

The colors used by the Iroquois were usually harmoniously blended, and strong contrasts were avoided. White beads surrounded colored beads, and were used between beads of contrasting colors, such as blue and pink, dark blue and yellow, light and dark purple, and red and light blue.

Wampum

Of the beads that were manufactured and used by the Iroquois, those known as "wampum" are by far the most significant. Though wampum broadly refers to discoidal and cylindrical beads, the true wampum is an Indian-made shell bead, cylindrical in form, and

Diorama of wampum being used in a council.

averaging about half a centimeter in length by three millimeters in diameter, perfectly straight on the side, each with a hole running through its length. Some of the wampum beads prepared for commercial trade were as long as a centimeter; however, none of the long beads have been found in the wampum belts. Wampum was made from the quahaug or hard shell clam, which provided both white and purple beads. The central axis of the great conch shell was used for white wampum.

Colored wampum had a special significance to the Iroquois. Colors ranged from pale pink and delicate lavender to deep purple. Purple beads were generally known as black wampum and were especially prized for political purposes. White was the emblem of purity and faith, and both pink and white wampum were symbolic of peace.

Wampum had several purposes. The first use of wampum was probably for personal adornment. Wampum beads were used in necklaces, collars, headbands, and armlets, and were sewn on articles of clothing. Until the end of the seventeenth century, the Iroquois also used wampum as money, either in strings or loose. It served as currency between the Indians and the Dutch and English colonists. In addition, wampum was used to pay the tribute deman-

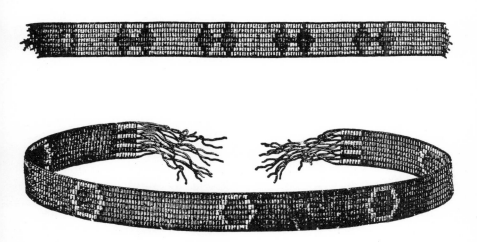

Onondaga wampum belts.

105

ded from the Iroquois by other tribes, and was also strung on cards for use in minor tribal transactions. Designs in a wampum belt recorded details of treaties and conveyed messages and condolences. It had special religious and social significance. Wampum also found its way into Iroquois legends, which mention a mythical wampum bird.

Wampum Strings and Belts

Both discoidal beads and cylindrical or true wampum beads were strung on nettle fibers or sinew to form wampum strings, several of which were usually tied together at one end in a bundle. Sometimes a special color arrangement was created in stringing the wampum in order to convey an intertribal message or to serve as a record in some minor tribal transaction. A string of invitation wampum was provided with small sticks or wooden handles at the ends, notched to indicate the number of days before the event. Wampum strings were sometimes bestowed by the clan matron when announcing the permanent name of an adult. Wampum belts were also used as seals of friendship following the ratification of treaties. Whites of the time had to be wary of an Indian council that did not bring forth and display its national wampums, and regarded it as either insincere or potentially dangerous.

Wampum belts were woven by a special technique using cylindrical beads on long strands of sinew, leather, vegetable fiber, or string. The various vegetable fibers on which wampum was strung included slippery elm, dogbane (also called black "Indian hemp" or amyroot), swamp milkweed, hairy milkweed (also called white "Indian hemp"), toad flax, and Indian mallow (popularly known as velvet leaf).

In preparation for belt making, both ends of the strands were inserted in a small piece of deer skin through holes spaced to keep the strands at equal distances from one another. The extreme ends of the strands were then fastened to either end of a piece of splint that had been sprung as a bow, allowing the strands to be held in tension as the warp. The beads that were to form the width of the belt were strung on a weft thread, traditionally of sinew, that was passed under the fiber strand in order to hold each bead lengthwise between the two strands, and at right angles to them. The thread was then passed back along the upper side of the strands and again through each bead so that it was held firmly in place by two threads, one passing over, and the other under, the strands. When the belt reached the desired length, the warp and weft strands were tied and the ends of the belt finished off, usually with a leather fringe. Belts varied from five or six beads in width to as many as fifty. Finished belts were usually from ten to fifteen centimeters wide and from thirty to 180 centimeters long. Old belts usually contained close to two thousand beads, although there were three thousand beads in the William Penn belt. Nearly ten thousand beads were used in one belt made by the Onondaga.

Many different designs appeared in the wampum belts. Designs woven in the belts included hollow squares, hexagons, diamonds, overlapping triangles, crosses, diagonal lines or bars, circles, hearts, pipes, houses, and human or animal figures. These were arranged in symbolic patterns, and their meaning was given by the maker of the

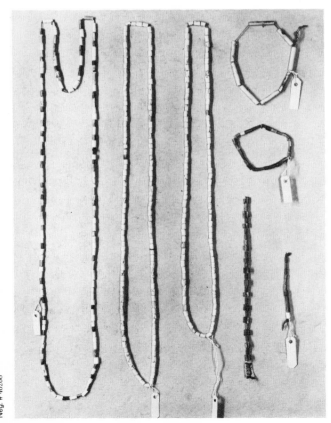

Department of Mines Geological Survey
Neg. # 40206

Wampum strings.

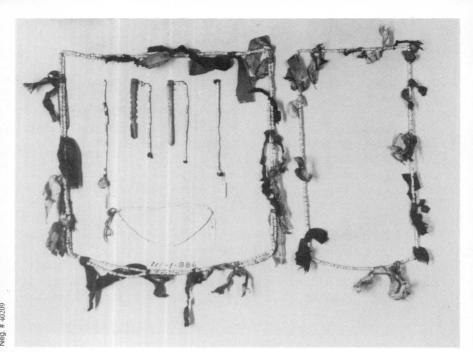

National Museum of Man
National Museums of Canada
Neg. # 40209

Wampum strings.

belt or was said to have been "talked into it" when a treaty was made.

Stories told by the designs served as reminders of tribal events. The belts were shown on regular ceremonial occasions, and the significance of the designs were explained. Some of the wampum belts were made only for temporary use, after which they were dismantled. Important belts, however, were preserved and were entrusted to a hereditary keeper versed in their interpretation.

The oldest wampum belt, known as the Hiawatha belt, is thought to date back to almost the middle of the sixteenth century, when it served to record the formation of the League of the Iroquois. The Hiawatha belt is today preserved, with twenty-four other important belts, in the State Museum at Albany, New York.

The Hiawatha belt's pattern shows four hollow squares outlined in white, and one white, heart-shaped design in the center, all of which are connected by white lines. These designs represent the five nations, with the great peace lodged in the heart. When reversed, the figure representing the heart assumes the appearance of a tree—the Great Tree of Light—under which the lines and the central heart were emblems of the peace, trust, charity, and justice that united the Five Nations.

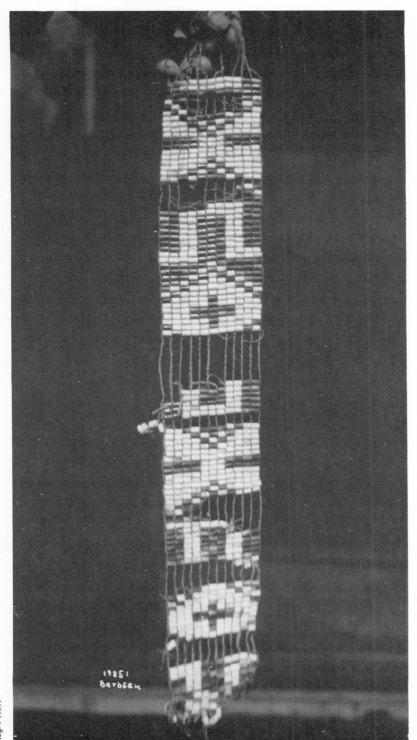

Department of Mines Geological Survey
Neg. # 19851

Wampum belt. Photo by C.M. Barbeau, 1911.

The Washington Covenant belt was used during the presidency of George Washington as a covenant of peace between the thirteen original colonies and the Six Nations of the Iroquois. It contains the symbolic figures of fifteen men with outstretched arms and clasped hands along its length. In the center is the figure of a house. The two figures on each side of the house are the Keepers of the East and the West Doors. Thirteen of the figures clasping hands represent the original colonies. The designs are woven in dark purple beads on a solid white beaded field that denotes peace and friendship.

The widest belt known, called the Wing or Dust Fan of Council President, shows a series of ten connecting purple, hexagonal figures on a white background. Both the figures and the background are edged with a white and a purple line of beads. The design is said to represent "The Evergrowing Tree," which symbolizes permanence and continuous growth of the League of the Iroquois. It was displayed whenever the League's constitution was recited to protect the Council, and to keep the eyes of the fifty civil rulers free from dust.

Another wide belt, sometimes called the Presidentia, has a design of overlapping purple triangles with a chain of fourteen white, open diamond-shaped figures along the central axis. The background is of white beads. At one time the belt was longer and there were sixteen diamonds, which represented a covenant, or a chain of friendship.

On an old wampum belt, known as the General Eli S. Parker belt, there are five dark purple, open hexagons outlined in white beads. Each symbolized the council of one of the nations of the League. Its white beads symbolized purity, peace, and integrity, and its dark purple beads symbolized royalty, dignity, and determination. This belt was originally known as the "five council fires," or "death belt" of the Five Iroquois Nations, and was long held by the Seneca, who guarded the west door of the League. It signified death or war against some nation or tribe and was sent from one nation of the confederacy to another when war was pending.

Eleven-strand wampum belt, in purple and white, from the Oka Reserve.

National Museum of Man

Wooden mask.

National Museum of Man
National Museums of Canada
Neg. #73999

SECRET SOCIETIES AND CEREMONIES

The tribal organization and national identity of each of the Six Nations was retained through the years because of the existence in each tribe of secret societies. Though societies varied in each tribe, the most generally known were the Secret Medicine Society, and the False Face Society. These were of ancient origin, and their rituals, in which dreams played an important role, were transmitted with little change for many years, especially among the Seneca. In the early history of the Iroquois it was taboo to recite rituals or chant songs to any but the initiated. Therefore, knowledge of the rituals of these societies was limited for some time.

Secret Medicine Society

The ceremonies of the Secret Medicine Society were usually calendrical, and were held to give thanks. Each one was appropriately named. The seven major festivals began with the mid-winter or New Year Festival, followed by the "Maple" or "Sap Dance" at the beginning of spring, the "Planting Festival" or "Seed Dance" (Soaking of the Seeds) in May, the "Berry Festival" or "Strawberry Dance," when the strawberries ripened, the "Green Bean Festival" or "String Bean Dance," when the string beans ripened, the "Green Corn Festival" or "Gathering of Food" at mid-year, and the "Harvest Festival" or "Bread Dance" in October, which showed gratitude for a good harvest.

A great deal of time was spent in preparation for and participation in ceremonies. Costumes, rattles, drums, canes, and other articles were assembled for each ceremony and thanksgiving festival. Feasting and merriment occurred during the afternoon and evening, when both religious and social dances were held. Enjoyment of life was considered to be a phase of thanksgiving. After the ceremonies were performed, the days were devoted to athletic contests between the tribes.

National Museum of Man
National Museums of Canada
Neg. # J-3171

False Face Society

The False Face ceremonies of the Iroquois were held for the purpose of exorcising evil spirits and driving away diseases. In the late fall and spring, members of the society went from house to house wearing masks and behaving like the spirits of the masks they represented, carrying rattles of horn, wood splints, hickory bark, or turtle shell.

Masks designed to be worn by members of the False Face Society were made in the image of a supernatural being. Brightly colored wooden masks depicting mythological and legendary characters, with grinning, hideous mouths, are known to have been used by the Seneca as far back as the seventeenth century. There were also many other types of masks representing different characters and serving different purposes. Corn husk masks were used by the Husk Face Society. Masks of buckskin were made to impersonate cannibal clowns who stole naughty children.

According to ancient legend, a strange creature in the form of a great head with terrible flaming eyes made his home on a huge rock, over which his long hair streamed. During storms the howling of the wind was thought to be his voice. Another legend told of several

National Museum of Man
National Museums of Canada
Neg. # J-3020

Dancer in false face mask with turtle shell rattle. Photo taken on the Iroquois reservation at Grand River, Ontario.

ugly, bodiless spirits who caused suffering and disease among the people. Iroquois legend also told of two brother heads, one red and one black, who had a half-red, half-black cousin. These legendary figures inspired the carving and use of the false face masks. Representations of the bear, the pig, and other animals are also seen in old masks.

Dance Customs

The Iroquois had many dances, most of which were associated with their ceremonies. Some of the dances were performed by selected dancers, who were attired in full costume and painted for the occasion. Frequently, both men and women participated in the dances.

The most popular dances were the War Dance, at which political speeches were made, and the Feather Dance, which was a

National Museum of Man
National Museums of Canada

Rain dance. Photo: C.M. Barbeau, 1949.

sacred worship of the Great Spirit. They were performed by a selected group of fifteen to thirty dancers who had distinguished themselves by their activity and powers of endurance.

Other ceremonial dances were named after the society that performed them. These included the False Face Dance, the Eagle Bear Dance, and Buffalo Dance, and dances named for a clan animal such as the duck, the fish, or the pigeon. These dances were held in the longhouse or in a field.

Music and song played an important part in the dances. The singers were seated in the center of the room and the dancers circled around them. Instruments used in the dances and songs included the turtle shell, gourd, or deer hoof rattles, feather wands, rhythm sticks, ceremonial whistles, and the water drum.

After the dances were over, such favorite foods as hulled corn soup and corn bread boiled with kidney beans were served by the feast-makers. These were either eaten on the spot or carried home in containers brought by each person.

Carved Masks

The carving of wooden masks was a ceremonial procedure, which was usually carried out by artists of exceptional ability. Masks varied according to the style of the artist who carved them, and were carved on the trunk of a living basswood, willow, cucumber, or other softwood tree in order to retain the potency and spirit of the tree. A three-day ceremony preceded the carving, during which sacred tobacco was burned, a pinch at a time, to beg forgiveness of the Tree Spirit for mutilating the tree. It was thought that blowing tobacco smoke into the roots and among the branches of the tree would allow it to heal over its scars in two to four years, and prevent it from dying. Later masks were often carved on barn beams.

The carving of masks followed one basic method. After the mask had been roughly blocked out, the entire block was cut off the tree, features were carefully carved in high relief, and the eyes were encircled with wide rings of sheet metal. The entire face was usually painted a solid black or red, according to the time of day the mask was carved. Masks on which carving was begun in the morning were painted red, while those begun after noon were painted black. A mask painted half-black and half-red was known as the whirlwind mask, because it was thought to have the power to divert an approaching storm. For this reason it was hung on trees facing the wind. Unpainted masks were worn by clowns. Long strands of basswood, moosewood, or slippery elm or black or white horehair were fastened to the top of the mask, and hung down to the knees of the wearer on both sides like hair. Tiny medicine bags were often attached to make the masks more potent.

Carving a wooden mask.
Photo: F.W. Waugh, 1912

Carved mask decorated with hair.

National Museum of Man
National Museums of Canada
Neg. # 18823, 73999

Carved wooden masks, of the False Face Society, decorated with hair and corn husks.

National Museum of Man
National Museums of Canada
Neg. # 73999

Masks were made in different sizes. Masks about twelve centimeters by eighteen centimeters were made for children. Miniature masks from three to eight centimeters in diameter, made of stone, wood, or corn husks, were attached to the larger masks, hung from the end of the leader's pole, or were used as charms to protect buildings. At one time the small mask was sent as a notification of election to candidates for admission to the False Face Society.

Corn Husk Masks

Members of the Husk Face Society, made up primarily of water doctors, wore corn husk masks originally made of braided strips of corn husks. These were sewn together in a distorted representation of the human face. In making the later corn husk masks, on the Alleghany reservation, a twined technique was used. Often the face was partially covered with a husk fringe, and closely resembled a husk mat. The face was sometimes carved of wood and surrounded by a thick corn husk fringe for hair. While wooden masks were carved by men, corn husk masks were made by women, and incorporated symbols of fertility and the harvest season.

There were two types of corn husk masks—braided and twined. To make a braided corn husk mask, three strips of tightly braided corn husks were coiled and a center hole was left in each coil—one for the mouth, and the other two for the eyes. To form the face, the coils were then sewn together with husk fiber or twine. A nose shaped from a piece of corn husk was added to complete the face. A twined corn husk mask was made by twining two weft fibers around warp fibers back and forth across the face of the mask, leaving openings for the eyes, nostrils, and mouth. Both types of masks were finished by the addition of eyebrows and a binding of braided or knotted husks, the loose ends of which were left to represent hair.

Husk masks were worn at the mid-winter ceremony, where the wearers of the masks acted as spirits of the harvest and appeared with digging sticks and hoes, performing a dance to inaugurate the

Iroquois corn husk masks.

National Museum of Man
National Museums of Canada
Neg. # 83740, 73995, 73996

Iroquois corn husk masks.

National Museum of Man
National Museums of Canada
Neg. #73995

new year. The masks were also used in the society's ceremonies at the time of the Green Corn Dance in the spring, and whenever help was given to someone in need so that the identity of the donor would not be known.

Ceremonial Whistles

The whistle or flute was called a *flageolet* by the Iroquois, and is thought to be an Indian invention. The first crude whistle of the Iroquois was made from the wing bone of a large bird. The later whistle, which resembled a clarinet, was usually made of red cedar, and was approximately forty-five centimeters in length, and a little over three centimeters in diameter. The six finger holes were equally spaced, but were closer to one end than the other. Between them and the mouthpiece at the far end was the whistle, which was much like a common whistle. The instrument sounded six consecutive notes from the bottom and three or four from the top, but the seventh note could not be sounded. When it was played by the Indians, this whistle afforded a kind of wild and plaintive music.

Water Drums

The bark water drum was used by the Iroquois for ceremonial occasions. It was from fifteen to thirty centimeters in diameter and from nine to eighteen centimeters high, and was usually made of a cedar or basswood log that was hollowed out to form a shell.

Sometimes two pieces of bark were shaped to form the drum. The bottom was made watertight with a perfectly fitting cross section of a log, which was carefully attached with spruce gum. Over the top, a piece of rawhide was tightly stretched and held firmly in place by an encircling rope of grapevine or vegetable fiber. A small hole was made in the side near the bottom of the drum and was stopped with a plug. When in use, the drum could be filled to different levels to produce a variety of tones. Drumsticks were very small and were sometimes ornately carved.

Rattles

The Iroquois were very resourceful in their creation of rattles. The turtle shell rattle was made by removing the body of the snapping turtle from its shell and replacing it with a handful of flint corn or cherry stones, then sewing up the opening. When it was to be used in the Feather Dance, designs were painted on the underside of the shell. The neck of the turtle was stretched over a corn stalk or short stick to form a handle.

Hollow squash shells, filled with corn, were also used as rattles. The sound varied according to the size of the squash. As many as twenty rattles, all of different tone, were sometimes used at once.

Man in false face mask with turtle shell rattle. Photo taken on the Iroquois reservation at Grand River, Ontario.

Neg. # J-3026

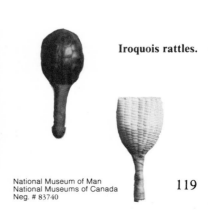

Iroquois rattles.

National Museum of Man
National Museums of Canada
Neg. # 83740

GAMES AND SPORTS

Games were played by the Iroquois as a part of their religious ceremonies, as an enjoyable pastime, and as a way to inspire a sense of competition. The Iroquois believed that games were pleasing to the Great Spirit, and they were often played with religious intent, particularly during a famine or epidemic, when a game might be ordered by the medicine men to appease the spirits. At the conclusion of sacred rituals, groups remained together to enjoy sports. In the early days of the League, games became contests between villages and tribes, and promoted the glorification of the winning team rather than the individual. Exhibitions of strength and skill were also held, and were very popular among the Iroquois.

Ball games, hoop games, and target shooting were popular summer sports. The most popular ball games among the Iroquois were lacrosse, shinny, and doubleball, the last two being played by girls and women. Foot races were often held, and long periods of practice usually preceded them. In winter showshoe races, shinny, iceball, snow snake, and snow boat were enjoyed, as well as indoor games of chance, which were played with various fruit stones, animal bones, or wooden articles. A great deal of time was spent by the men in the preparation of snowshoes, snow snakes, spears, javelins, lacrosse sticks, tallies, and other articles that were used in games.

**Playing cat's cradle.
Photo: F.W. Waugh, 1913.**

National Museum of Man
National Museums of Canada
Neg. # 17411

Ball Games

Doubleball was a game played by women. To play doubleball, two small buckskin bags were filled with sand and fastened together with a leather thong about one or two meters in length. A large group could play the game. Each player held a crooked stick with which the balls were tossed from player to player in an attempt to get them over the goal lines. The players were grouped into two teams and could intercept each other, catching the bags on their sticks and passing them on to their own goal line.

Another woman's game was known as shinny, and was very similar to fieldhockey. It was played with a flattened buckskin ball, whose opposite sides were painted in different colors. Each player, of which the number was unlimited, held a curved stick a little over a meter in length, which was sometimes painted or carved. The ball was driven by the stick only; hands could not be used.

Two poles serving as goals were set up about a meter apart at opposite ends of a field that was 180 or more meters long, and the participants were grouped into two opposing teams. The object of the game was to drive the ball through the goal of the other team. To play, the ball was placed in a shallow pit in the center of the field while the teams lined up just inside the goal posts. At a signal, both sides rushed to the center in an attempt to control the ball and drive it toward the goal of the other team.

Another ball game, lacrosse, was played by the Iroquois centuries prior to white contact. In ancient times a wooden ball, made from a burl or knot of wood, was used. Later a small ball of deer skin, stuffed hard with moss or hair and then sewn up with sinew, came into use. The original bat had a solid, curving head. Later, the bat was replaced by a curved stick strung with a net of sinew or deer skin thongs, which reached a point far up the handle. Because of its resemblance to a bishop's crozier, the racket was

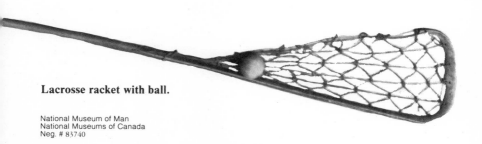

Lacrosse racket with ball.

National Museum of Man
National Museums of Canada
Neg. # 83740

called "la crosse" by the early French colonists, and the game came to be known as "lacrosse."

In preparation for the game, a large field or sheet of ice was cleared and "gates," consisting of two poles approximately three meters high, were erected about fifty-five meters apart at opposite ends of the field as goals. Before the game began each player removed all clothing except his breechcloth. The teams, of six or eight men each, assembled at each end and attempted to direct the ball with their rackets into the opponent's goal by knocking it on the ground, into the air, or by carrying it in the net of the racket. The game was fast paced, and usually lasted from noon until evening. Sometimes the contest was so close it was necessary to finish it on another day.

Making lacrosse rackets. Photo taken on the Iroquois reservation at Grand River, Ontario.

National Museum of Man
National Museums of Canada
Neg. # J-3111

National Museums of Canada
Neg. # J-2983

Iroquois boy demonstrating use of the lacrosse racket.

Games of Chance

Like other North American Indians, the Iroquois were fond of games of chance. There was a great variety of games, each having its different rules and special pieces of equipment. Dice games were played with wild plum or peach stones, cherry pits, beans, deer and elk horn or bone buttons, and carved wooden tally sticks or counters.

The peach stone or dish game was played with peach stones, which were filed or cut down to an oval shape so that they looked like smoothed-off hickory nuts. One side of each stone was slightly burned to blacken it. The game was played by placing six peach stones, with the same color facing up, in a flat-bottomed earthen or wooden dish carved out of a tree burl. After the dish was shaken violently, the stones were tossed on a pile of skins, and the number of pieces of each color exposed was counted. Red beans were used as scorekeeping counters. An equal number of beans was given to each side, and the game was played until one side had won all the beans.

The peach stone game was played three times a year in the longhouse—at the Indian New Year, the Maple Sugar Thanksgiving Festival, and the Green Corn Festival in September. Games sometimes lasted for several days.

Another game of chance was known as the deer button game. It

123

was played by two or more persons with eight buttons, each three centimeters in diameter, which were carved out of deer bone and blackened on one side. Sometimes the buttons were decorated with dots or with circular and radial designs. To play the game, the buttons were cupped in the hands and thrown down, usually on a blanket. The relative number of black and white faces turned up determined the points scored. The game continued until one player had won fifty beans.

The ring, or cup and pin, game was played with seven conical bones loosely strung on a leather thong, which was about twenty centimeters in length. The bones were usually smaller at one end and could be slipped into one another. At one end of the thong was a small piece of fur and at the other was a hickory stick nine centimeters long. The game was played by holding the stick in the hand, swinging the bones upward, and trying to insert the pointed end of the stick into one or more of the bones as they were descending. Each bone had a value of its own, the highest value being on the lowest bone. The player who totaled up the highest score was the winner.

Hoop Games

Hoop games were played with shooting sticks, poles, spears, and javelins. Hoops of different sizes were made of bent, unpeeled saplings, usually of hickory or maple, which were tied around the overlapping ends with bark. Some of the hoops were filled with an elaborate hexagonal weaving. Spears varied in size from small darts to poles 4½ meters long.

The javelin used in the hoop and javelin game was 150 to 180 centimeters in length and two centimeters in diameter, and was usually made of hickory or maple. It was sharpened at one end, finished with care, and striped spirally. The hoop used was twenty centimeters in diameter and was either left open or filled with netting. Sometimes the javelin was thrown horizontally by placing a forefinger at its end and supporting it with the thumb and second finger; in other cases it was held in the center and thrown with the hand raised above the shoulder. The game was played by fifteen to thirty players with three to six javelins apiece, who were arranged on each of two sides according to tribal divisions. While one team rolled hoops along a center line, the other team attempted to throw their javelins through the hoops. Players who missed had to forfeit their javelins to the other side. The game was won by the team that could throw the greatest number of javelins through the hoops as they rolled.

The hoop and dart game was played with a hoop made of a sapling, and darts 120 to 150 centimeters in length. Players lined up about three meters apart, usually with two darts apiece. A member of one side threw the hoop so that it went spinning along the ground rapidly, while the other side launched their darts at it. The object was to hit and stop the hoop as it rolled by. If a player missed, his dart was forfeited, but if it went under the hoop he retained it.

The hoop and pole game was played with a hoop made of an unpeeled bent sapling tied with bark forty centimeters in diameter, and six poles slightly over two meters in length. Five or six persons played. While the hoop was rolled, all the players threw their poles. The player whose pole stopped the ring owned it. The others then shot in turn, having to forfeit those poles that missed to the owner of the hoop. The owner of the hoop then took all the forfeited poles and shot them at the hoop, winning those that he put through it. If two men stopped the hoop, the poles were divided between them.

Boys using throwing sticks. Photo: F.W. Waugh, 1912.

National Museums of Canada
Neg. # 17165

Snow Snake

Snow snake, which may be called the national game of the Iroquois, was a popular winter sport. Snow snakes were smooth, polished, flexible rods made from various kinds of hardwood, such as maple, walnut, or hickory. They were from 150 to 275 centimeters in length and three centimeters in diameter at the head, tapering to about one centimeter at the tail. A slight notch was made near the small end, or the upper surface was left slightly concave, to allow for a better finger hold. The head was rounded and turned up slightly on the underside like the fore part of a skate runner. Later, the head was weighted with lead to help its balance. The snow snake was made with precision and given a fine finish. When there had been a good snowfall, a smooth, shallow course was laid out on a level stretch, sometimes slightly sloping. A smooth-barked log was pulled in a straight line through the track for 450 to 600 meters. This packed the snow, making a trough twenty-five to forty-five centimeters deep. The course was then sprinkled with water to form an ice crust. Players gathered at one end of the track and in turn threw the snow snakes, each attempting to make them travel the longest distance possible in the shortest time. Before it was thrown, the snake was rubbed with a skin saturated with secret "medicine" (oil or wax). The player grasped the snake firmly in his hand, placed his forefinger in the notch that had been cut in the tail, and, balancing with his left hand, stooped toward the ground with the snake held horizontally over the course. Then with a few quick, short steps he threw the snake with considerable force along the

Shooting snow snakes. Photo: F.W. Waugh, 1912.

National Museum of Man
National Museums of Canada
Neg. # 20239

course. The snake traveled with the speed of an arrow, sometimes for a distance of 300 or 400 meters. Goal markers indicated where each snake stopped. Victory was awarded the player or team that had thrown four or more snakes over the greatest distance in a specified number of attempts.

Target Shooting and Arrow Throwing

Target shooting was carried out by the Iroquois with a bow and arrow. The bow was just over a meter long and had a powerful spring, which was extremely difficult for the inexperienced person to draw. It could shoot an arrow with great force. Arrows were ninety centimeters long and feathered at the small end with a twist, which made them spin while in flight. Every man had his arrows marked so that he could identify them. Originally the arrows were pointed with a piece of flint, horn, bone, or chert, which made them exceedingly dangerous missiles, as they could deeply penetrate any object they hit.

Arrows were sometimes thrown by hand. Arrow throwing was a skill requiring speed and strength. The winner of the game was the person who threw the greatest number of single arrows into the air before the first one thrown could fall to the ground.

Use of the bow and arrow. Photo has been taken just as the arrow is being released. Photo: F.W. Waugh, 1912.

National Museum of Man
National Museums of Canada
Neg. # 42720

127

CONCLUSION

Though Iroquois arts show many distinctive features, the close relation of their work to that of other Woodland Indians is apparent. Iroquois bark containers, basketry, quillwork, beadwork, woven yarn sashes, and ribbonwork all show the influence of other Woodland tribes. However, the elaborate development of unique designs, such as the much-used scroll pattern, gives Iroquois clothing and accessories a characteristic finish that makes them easily recognizable. Other crafts, such as the carved wooden masks of the False Face Society, and the snow snakes, which were used in a game that was unique to the Iroquois, gave an identity to these tribes. Their agricultural leanings were reflected in their many corn husk and cob products, including the masks made by the Husk Face Society.

The most impressive achievement of the Iroquois, their political organization, was recorded and represented by their crafts. Wampum and other symbolic arts related directly to League politics and society, and helped to distinguish the Iroquois stylistically and culturally from the other Woodland tribes.

Braiding corn husks for mats. Photo: F.W. Waugh, 1912.

National Museum of Man
National Museums of Canada
Neg. # 18815